Internet Exercises

for use with

Advertising and Promotion
An Integrated Marketing Communications Perspective

Fourth Edition

George E. Belch
San Diego State University

Michael A. Belch
San Diego State University

Prepared by
Joshua Pincus

Irwin McGraw-Hill

Boston   Burr Ridge, IL   Dubuque, IA   Madison, WI   New York   San Francisco   St. Louis
Bangkok   Bogotá   Caracas   Lisbon   London   Madrid
Mexico City   Milan   New Delhi   Seoul   Singapore   Sydney   Taipei   Toronto

Irwin/McGraw-Hill

A Division of The McGraw·Hill Companies

Internet Exercises to accompany
ADVERTISING AND PROMOTION:
AN INTEGRATED MARKETING COMMUNICATIONS PERSPECTIVE

1 2 3 4 5 6 7 8 9 0 BBC/BBC 9 0 9 8 7

ISBN 0-07-012291-1

http://www.mhhe.com

TABLE OF CONTENTS

INTRODUCTION

OVERVIEW

Welcome to the *Internet Exercises to accompany **Advertising and Promotion***, 4th edition, by Belch and Belch. The purpose of this exercise book is threefold:

- To help students explore and understand the marketing concepts and practices featured in the main text by applying them to real-world examples on the World Wide Web.

- To provide students with a wide array of activities and exercises through which they can develop their World Wide Web navigation and research skills.

- To engage students in a critical examination of the World Wide Web as an integrated marketing communications (IMC) tool by asking them to evaluate hundreds of Websites and devise their own creative ways of applying this dynamic medium.

This introduction is intended to provide a concise overview of the World Wide Web (or Web, for short), how it works, and how it fits into the "big picture" of the Internet. The emphasis here is on the practical rather than the technical. To fully demonstrate the electronic complexities of the Web would require a technical discussion that is well beyond the scope of this course. In the next few pages we will explain — in everyday language wherever possible — the essential Web technology and terminology you will need to understand in order to make the most of this exercise book.

WHAT IS THE WORLD WIDE WEB?

Let's approach this question by first establishing what the **World Wide Web** is *not*. One common misconception is that the Web and the Internet are one and the same. They are not. The term **Internet** refers to the physical infrastructure of an interconnected global computer network. In effect, the Internet is just a giant mass of cables and computers. The Internet itself doesn't do anything. To make the most of this physical network, software engineers have developed programs and protocols that allow these computers to communicate with each other in different ways. The Web refers to just one of many modes of data storage and transfer commonly used on the Internet (e-mail and Usenet being two other examples, both of which we will cover in later sections).

On the most basic level, the Web is just a vast collection of interconnected documents stored on computers all around the world. These computers, or **hosts**, must be connected to the Internet, of course. A special coding system called Hypertext Mark-Up Language, or **HTML**, allows Web users to move quickly and easily within and between documents. An individual user navigates through these HTML-encoded documents with a software program called a **browser**. The browser interprets the HTML codes in two ways. First, it uses these codes to format and display the text and images you see on your screen (the codes themselves remain hidden). Secondly, it executes the appropriate commands whenever your click on any given highlighted text, or **hypertext link**. Furthermore, recent advancements in HTML now allow users to click on pictures and animation, or **hypermedia**, in order to execute these same commands.

BROWSERS

In order to understand how a browser works, it is helpful to look at the **client/server system** upon which the Web is built. When you use the Web, you are using two programs, the client and the server. The **client** program, or browser, is the program running on your local terminal, whether it's your PC at home or a UNIX workstation at school. It displays information on your screen, responds to your keystrokes and mouse clicks, and retrieves the information you request. It retrieves this information (which may consist of text, graphics, animation, sound, and even movies!) from the host computer, or **server**, which is connected to the Internet. The important thing to note here is that the server does nothing until it receives a command from the browser.

Currently, the most popular browsers are Microsoft's Internet Explorer and Netscape's Navigator, though many other software packages are also available. Internet Explorer may be downloaded for free (www.microsoft.com) or ordered directly from Microsoft for a nominal fee. The single-user version of Navigator (now part of a larger package called Communicator) can be purchased from a software retailer or downloaded directly from the Internet (www.netscape.com), but it is offered free of charge to the educational community — that means you! Multi-user versions for local computer networks are also available through a site license. If you are using Netscape (or any other browser) on a terminal in your school's computer center, odds are it's a multi-user version.

WEBSITES & HOMEPAGES

Using your browser, you can access homepages and Websites all over the world. While these two terms are often used interchangeably, the term **Website** actually refers to an entire collection of HTML documents stored on a given server. The term **homepage** denotes the main access point (or "front door") into this collection. A typical homepage will describe the purpose and features of the Website and provide an interactive table of contents that serves as the navigation scheme for the Website as a whole. For example, the Arizona State University Website consists of many different areas (academic, administrative, reference, campus life, etc.), all of which appear as hypertext or hypermedia links on the main homepage. To make things a little more complicated, each of these areas or departments may have their own servers and homepages. Open the front door and you'll find more doors (behind which are even more doors!). Some of these doors lead to other documents on the same Website, while others may lead to different Websites all over the world. This maze-like effect is how the World Wide Web got its name.

UNIFORM RESOURCE LOCATORS (URLs)

Uniform Resource Locators, or URLs, are what we use to get our bearings within this maze. Put simply, a URL is the Internet address of a given Website, homepage, or document. What's more, URLs can tell you exactly where specific documents are located within a particular Website.

URLs consist of four parts. We'll use the following URL as an example:

http://www.asu.edu/asuweb/indext.html

- The first part, **http://**, which is referred to as the *prefix*, indicates that this address points to an HTML-encoded document (http stands for Hypertext Transport Protocol). Therefore, you know it's a Website. Other prefixes you may run across in your Web travels include ftp://, file://, gopher://, and telnet://. All of the URLs in this exercise book point to Web documents, so the only prefix you'll see here is http://. The other prefixes listed above serve as a reminder that browsers can be used to access Internet resources other than Web documents.

- The second part, **www.asu.edu**, is the name of the computer (or host or server) where this document is stored. Another term for this label is *domain name*. In this example, the computer is Arizona State University's primary Web server.

- The third part, **/asuweb/**, is the directory on this server where the file resides.

- The fourth part, **index.html**, is the name of the actual document that appears on your screen. This document may contain text, graphics, animation, sound files, movies, and/or hyperlinks to other documents and Websites.

It is especially advantageous to know the common abbreviations that are used in the naming of particular servers. In the above example, the domain name ends with *.edu*, signifying that the computer is part of an educational or research institution. The other standard suffixes in current use are as follows:

.com	Commercial organizations
.gov	Government agencies
.mil	Military agencies
.net	Major network support centers
.org	Not-for-profit organizations
.int	International organizations

Information may be interpreted differently depending on whether it comes from a commercial, government, military, or other source, so it is important to know these abbreviations and always be conscious of where you are on the Web.

SEARCHING THE WEB

Now that you know a bit about the Web's addressing scheme, how can you find what you're looking for on this vast information network? Our first suggestion may surprise you: GUESS! This method is especially useful for finding company and university Websites, as illustrated in the following examples.

Let's say you want to find the homepage for Cornell University. You already know that **http://** is the prefix for Web documents, so that will be the first part of its URL. By far the most common beginning for a Web server domain name is **www**, so that's another safe bet for the next piece of the URL. And you already know that since Cornell is an educational institution, the domain will end in **edu**. The last element to fill in is the name of the school itself, **Cornell**, which is the middle element of the domain name (the word "university" is usually omitted in cases like this). Put it all together and you get **http://www.cornell.edu**, which is, in fact, the main URL for Cornell University.

The same logic can be applied to corporate Websites. Can you guess the Xerox Website URL? The prefixes will be the same as above, but you know that the domain name will end in *.com* because Xerox is a commercial organization. Fill in the company name and you get http://www.xerox.com. The same logic can be applied to guessing the Website addresses for government sites (like the White House at http://www.whitehouse.gov) and not-for-profit organizations (like Greenpeace at http://www.greenpeace.org).

If this method doesn't help you find what you're looking for, you can also try one of the many **search engine** Websites available on the Internet. A significant number of the exercises in this book ask you to use these remarkable tools, so you will get plenty of practice with search engines as you work your way through these exercises.

Search engines are some of the most powerful and utilized resources on the Web. These enormous interactive databases allow us to scour most of Webspace in a matter of seconds in search of just about anything. There are more than a dozen comprehensive search engines on the Web, including:

Alta Vista	http://www.altavista.digital.com
Excite!	http://www.excite.com
Infoseek	http://www.infoseek.com
Lycos	http://www.lycos.com
Magellan	http://www.mckinley.com
Open Text Index	http://index.opentext.com
WebCrawler	http://www.webcrawler.com
Yahoo!	http://www.yahoo.com
ZD Net	http://www.zdnet.com

At the most basic level, there are two ways to find what you're looking for…

First, there is the **keyword search**. Each search engine is a little different, but the general idea is that you input words related to the information you are looking for and the engine will give you a list of sites containing those words. So if you are trying to find a hotel for your next trip to Miami, you might try words like *Miami, Florida, travel, tourism, hotels,* etc. In general, the more specific you can be, the better. Each search engine has a comprehensive Help or Search Tips menu that can make your research much more efficient (and much less frustrating). We encourage you to take advantage of these useful guides.

Secondly, some of these search engines feature **hierarchical databases**. This means that you may navigate these Websites by choosing from a list of general topic areas and narrowing your search from there (Yahoo! is the best known example of this structure). Thus, the above search might go something like this: Recreation → Travel → United States → Southeast Region → Florida → Miami → Lodging.

OTHER FEATURES OF THE INTERNET — E-MAIL & USENET NEWS

Besides the Web, two other features of the Internet are mentioned in this exercise book — e-mail and Usenet news.

Electronic mail, or **e-mail**, is the primary communication tool used on the Internet. E-mail is a system for sending messages and/or files to the accounts of other computer users. The sender and recipient(s) may be on the same computer or on different systems on opposite sides of the world. E-mail works very much like regular postal mail. Every user on the network has a private mailbox. Once received, your mail is kept for you until you decide to discard it. Like regular postal mail, you must know a user's address to send a message. This communication technology is being used more and more for direct marketing, which is the focus of the e-mail exercises in this book.

Usenet, or Netnews, is a worldwide electronic bulletin board system. It represents a way for people with similar interests to communicate with one another by exchanging publicly posted messages known as *articles*. Unlike e-mail messages, which are delivered straight to your private mailbox, Usenet articles are posted to a central computer known as a *news server*, where anyone with access may read and respond to them (either privately or publicly). Each news server is divided into *newsgroups*, which are categorized by topic area. For example, the rec.music.folk newsgroup is for fans of folk music. The *rec* prefix indicates that this is a recreational group. Other prefixes include *comp* (for computer topics), *sci* (for scientific discussion) and *K12* (for students in kindergarten through 12th grade). Like e-mail, Usenet is changing the way people communicate, so it is an important medium for marketers to understand.

COMMERCIAL ONLINE SERVICES VS. THE INTERNET

One of the most common sources of confusion with respect to the Internet is the unique position occupied by major commercial online services such as America Online, CompuServe, and Prodigy. Many newcomers to the information superhighway (often called "newbies") assume that these services are synonymous with the Internet. They are not. These networks are independent systems offering a wide variety of informational, entertainment, commercial, and other resources, only one of which is access to the wider, global system we call the Internet (including the Web). While subscribers to these systems can access the Internet, non-subscribers cannot access these systems' internal services. It is important to understand this distinction when considering the Internet, and more specifically the Web, as a marketing medium.

OTHER FEATURES OF THIS EXERCISE BOOK

A few other features of this supplement deserve mention at this point. First, just as in the main text, key terms appear in boldface type. Secondly, each exercise is accompanied by a page reference to relevant material in the main text. These references appear to the right of the descriptive title for each exercise. Finally, we have provided an index of all the Websites featured in this supplement. This index is arranged by business area and includes corresponding exercise numbers for each Website.

The author wishes to thank Natalie Hewitt for her invaluable support and input throughout the development of this exercise book.

Chapter 1: AN INTRODUCTION TO INTEGRATED MARKETING COMMUNICATIONS

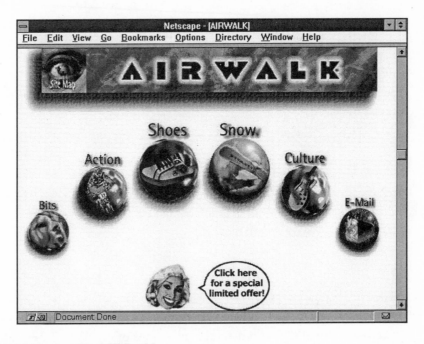

1-1   AIRWALK vs. AIR JORDAN   (3)

a)   As you read in the chapter-opening vignette, Airwalk has claimed a significant percentage of the athletic footwear market by promoting a company and product image that is in tune with its target audience — namely, youths ages 7 to 25. The authors have pointed out a few ingredients in Airwalk's recipe for "coolness." To further explore this timely **marketing** strategy, walk yourself through the Airwalk Website and answer the following questions:

     Airwalk   http://www.airwalk.com

How does Airwalk use this homepage to further its "cool" and youthful image? In particular, identify and describe those elements that have little or nothing to do with the shoes themselves. What does this tell us about what Airwalk is really selling? Do you think that the Web is an effective medium for reaching Airwalk's target audience? Why or why not?

b)   Now take a look at the homepage for one of Airwalk's biggest competitors, Reebok:

     Reebok   http://www.reebok.com

How does this Website differ from Airwalk's in terms of the image, style, and fashion? That is, how does Reebok seem to define "cool"? Based on what you see here, how would you describe Reebok's target audience?

1-2   GLOBAL PERSPECTIVE: REACHING CUSTOMERS AROUND THE WORLD   (6)

a)   Like Microsoft (see Global Perspective 1-1), Nissan Motor Company's growth strategy places heavy emphasis on expanding international markets. You can see this for yourself by visiting the Website maintained at Nissan headquarters in Japan:

> Nissan Motor Co. (Japan)   http://www.nissan.co.jp

Take the "Global CyberCruise" to get a general sense of Nissan's global orientation. Compare and contrast the various regional homepages. How can you account for the variation among these presentations? What common threads can you identify?

b)   Now take a look at the Nissan USA homepage:

> Nissan USA   http://www.nissan-usa.com

How does this site differ from those you perused in the first part of this exercise? How do you account for these differences? Do you think that the Nissan USA Web **advertising** campaign would be effective in other countries? Why or why not?

1-3   RELATIONSHIP MARKETING   (6-7)

Relationship marketing is one of the most natural applications of the Web. Internet technology allows companies to promote long-term relationships with customers (and other stakeholders) by offering product-related services, resources, and activities *online*. These efforts go well beyond standard customer support. Identify and describe the ways in which each of the following Websites embody a relationship marketing orientation:

> The New York Yankees   http://www.yankees.com
> Ragu Foods   http://www.ragu.com
> The Discovery Channel   http://www.discovery.com

Which aspects of the Web medium (and the Internet as a whole) make it especially well-suited to relationship marketing?

1-4   INTRODUCING INTEGRATED MARKETING COMMUNICATIONS   (8-12)

The advertising department at the University of Texas has created an extensive directory of marketing communication resources called Advertising World. You can find this invaluable resource at the following URL (we suggest you bookmark this site for future use):

> Advertising World   http://advweb.cocomm.utexas.edu/world

One of the many features of this site is a tremendous collection of advertising agency links (click on Advertising Agencies). Choose three of these agencies and familiarize yourself with their operations by perusing their homepages. Based on what you find, determine whether or not each company reflects an **integrated marketing communications (IMC)** approach. For those that do, identify and describe those services and/or programs that reflect this orientation. That is, use each IMC company you have identified to illustrate the critical components of IMC. For those that do not, explain why they do not fit this description and outline what it would take for them to become an IMC agency.

1-5   IMC PERSPECTIVE: CHANGING ATTITUDES TOWARD MILK   (13-21)

a) As you read in IMC Perspective 1-3 (p. 15), phase one of the "Milk, Where's Your Mustache?" campaign was executed exclusively through magazine advertisements. Since then, Bozell Worldwide (the agency behind the ads) has added Web advertising to its campaign strategy. Check out the following homepage and answer the questions below:

"Milk, Where's Your Mustache?"   http://www.whymilk.com

Identify and describe the ways in which this homepage differs from the magazine ads you have seen. Which of the **promotional mix** elements presented here do not appear in the print ads? In general, what does this demonstrate about the relative advantages and disadvantages of Web advertising versus traditional print advertising?

b) How does this campaign compare to the famous "got milk?" TV commercials (sponsored by a different dairy industry group) you have seen? How would you characterize the central message or theme of each campaign?

Next, take a look at the "got milk?" Website:

"got milk?"   http://www.got-milk.com

How does this homepage differ from the other "got milk?" advertising you have seen in other media? How do you account for these differences?

c) Would you classify the Web as a *mass media*? Explain. Do you think that the Web is an effective and worthwhile medium for campaigns like "Milk, Where's Your Mustache?" and "got milk?"? Why or why not? (Recall that Bozell originally opted not to run TV ads because they were too expensive and the ads might have gotten lost among all the other beverage commercials.)

Finally, why will it be difficult to measure the effectiveness of these campaigns?

1-6   ADVERTISING TO CONSUMER MARKETS   (16)

Figure 1-3 presents a general classification system for advertising to both consumer and business/professional markets. As you explore the following Websites, list and describe all of the ways in which each advertising effort corresponds to this classification system. (*Note*: an individual homepage may fall into more than one category.)

Stora	http://www.stora-paperboard.com
California Tomatoes	http://www.tomato.org
Advanstar Healthcare Publishing	http://www.modernmedicine.com
Sayville Ford	http://www.fordgiant.com
Interactive Intelligence	http://www.inter-intelli.com/resellers.html
Nabisco	http://www.nabisco.com

1-7   PUBLICITY/PUBLIC RELATIONS   (20)

The Web represents an inexpensive and convenient channel through which organizations can distribute their news releases. Not only can they feature these items on their own homepages, but they can funnel them through a number of news release sites such as the Yahoo! PR Newswire.

Yahoo! PR Newswire   http://biz.yahoo.com/prnews

As you peruse the PR Newswire, answer the following questions:

Would you classify news releases as **publicity** or **public relations**? Explain your answer.

Pick two items from today's PR Newswire that are of interest to you, but which are different from each other (i.e., representing two different industries). Print out both releases and summarize the central message of each one. Would you describe these releases as *proactive* or *reactive*? Explain. Where else might you expect to find these items? What are the advantages and disadvantages of this kind of **promotion** (versus advertising, **direct marketing**, etc.)?

How does the Web compare to other media as a new release distribution channel? Again, what are the advantages and disadvantages of the various channels?

1-8   SITUATION ANALYSIS: EXTERNAL FACTORS   (26-7)

First, identify a specific product or product type that you know well and/or use regularly — perhaps one related to a hobby or recreational activity you enjoy. This product should be familiar and interesting to you. Next, using one of the search engines below (if necessary), locate the Website for a company that manufactures and/or sells this product (preferably a company you have done business with in the past):

Yahoo!	http://www.yahoo.com
Alta Vista	http://www.altavista.digital.com
Excite!	http://www.excite.com

Using your prior knowledge of this product along with the Website you found, summarize the process you might go through if you were a marketing executive for this company and you wanted to perform an external situation analysis. What are the relevant external factors? Using Figure 1-5 as a guide, try to answer (or at least describe how you would approach answering) the questions central to the customer, competitive, and environmental analyses. Which questions are most difficult to answer? Which are the easiest?

Finally, how would you expect the results of this analysis to influence (1) your marketing strategy in general and (2) your company's Website in particular?

1-9   MARKETING OBJECTIVES vs. COMMUNICATION OBJECTIVES   (27)

A crucial part of the **promotional planning** process is establishing communication goals and objectives. The authors stress the importance of distinguishing between **communication objectives** and **marketing objectives**. Identify and describe both the communication and marketing objectives evidenced in the following homepages:

U.S. Army Recruiting	http://www.goarmy.com
San Diego Zoo	http://www.sandiegozoo.org
Union Carbide	http://www.unioncarbide.com
Jenny Craig	http://www.jennycraig.com

1-10   CREATIVE STRATEGY vs. MEDIA STRATEGY   (28)

Use the following homepage to illustrate the difference between creative strategy and media strategy. Be sure to identify the primary sponsors of this cooperative Website and describe how each stands to benefit from its success. What does this demonstrate about the relationship between creative strategy and media strategy?

UnfURLed	http://www.unfurled.com

Chapter 2: THE ROLE OF IMC IN THE MARKETING PROCESS

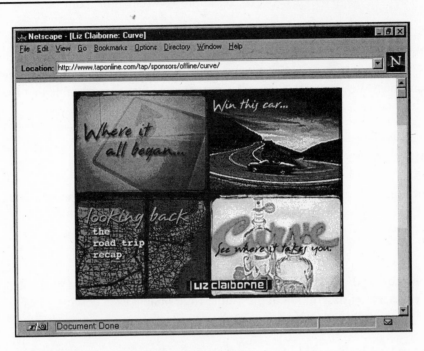

2-1   LIZ CLAIBORNE'S CURVE ON THE WEB   (33)

a) Liz Claiborne contracted MarketSource Interactive (MSI) to develop and execute an online promotional campaign for Curve. Before we take a look at the Curve homepage itself, let's visit the MarketSource corporate Website:

> MarketSource Corp./   http://www.marketsource.com
> MarketSource Interactive

Considering what you know about the target market for Curve, why do you think Liz Claiborne chose MarketSource for this campaign? Would you describe MarketSource as an IMC firm? Explain.

b) To access the Curve homepage, follow MarketSource's <u>Interactive</u> link and choose the <u>Success</u> option (this option may also be called "Featured Clients" or something similar). This will reveal a list of MSI's clients and a brief description of each interactive project. Click on <u>Liz Claiborne</u> to see what they developed for Curve.

How is this Website consistent with the other promotional mix elements described in the chapter-opening vignette? What are the relative advantages and disadvantages of this Website compared to the traditional advertising media (i.e., print, outdoor, radio, and TV) chosen for this campaign?

(exercise continued on following page...)

c) As this exercise book went to press, the only Website through which one could access the Curve homepage was the t@p online network, another of MSI's clients. t@p online can be found at the following URL:

t@p online network   http://www.taponline.com

Write a brief description of t@p online (i.e., what is it?). How does t@p online fit into the overall Curve marketing strategy? What are the advantages and disadvantages of relying exclusively on a service like t@p online to attract new customers via the Web— as opposed to maintaining a free-standing, independent Website? (Note: by the time you read this, it is possible that Liz Claiborne will have established such an independent site. If so, check it out!)

2-2   GLOBAL PERSPECTIVE: COKE VS. PEPSI ON THE WEB   (38)

To see how the cola wars are being played out on the Web, take a look at the following Websites:

The Coca-Cola Co.   http://www.cocacola.com
Pepsi World   http://www.pepsi.com

As you can see, these soft-drink giants have put together two of the most sophisticated Websites on the Internet. Write a brief description of the online environment each company has developed. What kind of image, style, and fashion does each site reflect?

Based on what you see here, would you say that Coke and Pepsi are targeting the same market segment(s)? Explain. Do these Websites seem to address a different market segment(s) than their other mass media campaigns (i.e., TV, radio, print, outdoor)? If so, how do you account for this difference? If not, list and describe the major themes that are consistent across the various mass media for each company.

Finally, describe the international component of each Website. How are Coke and Pepsi using the Web to develop global markets (if at all)? Why is the Web a potentially effective marketing tool for reaching markets outside the US? Conversely, what are its major limitations in this area?

2-3   IDENTIFYING TARGET MARKETS   (39-40)

Both of the following Websites promote products and/or services that have been divided into distinct target **market segments**:

Holiday Inn Hotels   http://www.holiday-inn.com
Kellogg Co.   http://www.kelloggs.com

For each company, create an outline summarizing the various market segments evidenced in these homepages. On which parameters are these segments based (i.e., social class, lifestyle, taste, etc.)? Be sure to address all the need satisfaction variables that apply in each case.

a) Exercise 2-3 demonstrated how a large firm can use **market segmentation** to diversify its product mix and thereby target more clearly defined customer populations. Now let's take a look at how a handful of companies are attempting to carve up the overall market for a product most of us use every day — wristwatches:

Timex	http://www.timex.com
Omega	http://www.omega.ch
Swatch	http://www.swatch.com
Vision Watch	http://www.visionwatch.com

Using the above Websites for reference, describe the market segment(s) targeted by each of the above wristwatch manufacturers. How are these segments reflected in the content and style of each homepage? Between which of these companies would you expect to find the most market segment overlap (i.e., the most competition)?

b) Obviously, there are dozens of other wristwatch manufacturers competing in these arenas. Using the Yahoo! search engine (http://www.yahoo.com), locate the Website for a wristwatch manufacturer not on the above list. How would you describe its market segmentation strategy? Which of the above companies would it compete with most? What does this demonstrate about the challenges marketers face in developing effective segmentation strategies?

2-5   BASES FOR SEGMENTATION   (41-5)

a) The authors present five different **bases for market segmentation**: **geographic**, **demographic**, **psychographic**, **behavioristic**, and **benefit**. Using illustrations from the Websites listed below, describe how these segmentation schemes can be applied to the following health and beauty products:

Oral-B	http://www.oralb.com
Urban Decay	http://www.urbandecay.com
Just for Men	http://www.justformen.com

(*Note*: keep in mind that certain bases will be easier to apply than others in each case.)

b) Which one of the five bases for segmentation applies most directly to each of the following companies? Explain your choice in each case.

Safe-T-Proof	http://www.safe-t-proof.com
BET Networks	http://www.betnetworks.com
Accessability Travel	http://www.disabled-travel.com
Cellular One	http://www.cellularone.com

15

2-6   PSYCHOGRAPHIC SEGMENTATION: VALS 2 (41-3)

The Stanford Research Institute (SRI) maintains a unique and useful Website called the Business Intelligence Center, which you will find at the following URL:

Business Intelligence Center   http://future.sri.com

a)   This Website features a wealth of resources related to SRI's Values and Lifestyles Program, or VALS 2. Once you have connected to this site, choose the <u>VALS 2</u> link. At this point, you will be given the opportunity to type yourself according to the VALS 2 segmentation system by completing a simple questionnaire. After you have completed the questionnaire and received your results, answer the following questions.

Which of the eight lifestyle groups were you assigned to? Based on SRI's description of your primary lifestyle group, do you agree with your results? That is, do you feel that this category accurately reflects your lifestyle? If so, how? If not, why not?

Familiarize yourself with all eight of the VALS 2 lifestyle groups. Do you think this is a fair and useful classification system? What are its limitations? What are the potential pitfalls of using a questionnaire to determine psychographic segmentation?

b)   Finally, locate and follow the <u>iVALS</u> (Internet VALS) link. Similar to VALS 2, iVALS was specifically designed as a segmentation system for the Internet population — that is, Web users like you. Just as you did before, complete the iVALS questionnaire and critically analyze your results. Do you believe that the iVALS segmentation system is a fair and useful reflection of the Internet population? Again, discuss the limitations and pitfalls of a classification scheme such as this.

2-7   DETERMINING HOW MANY SEGMENTS TO ENTER (47)

In determining how many segments to enter, three marketing coverage alternatives are available: **undifferentiated marketing**, **differentiated marketing**, and **concentrated marketing**. Determine which one of these three approaches applies most directly to each of the following companies. Explain your answers.

Micro-flo Industries	http://www.micro-flo.com
Bugle Boy	http://www.bugleboy.com
Energizer	http://www.energizer.com

Given what you know about the current competitive environment, which of the above coverage alternatives do you think is the least common? Why? (If you're not sure how to answer this question, try to think of a few real-world examples for each alternative. Which category gave you the most trouble?)

Identify and briefly describe the **positioning** strategies embodied in the following Websites. Use specific examples from each site to support your answer. Again, more than one positioning strategy may be at work in each case, so be sure to address all that apply.

DISH Network	http://www.dishtv.com
Ziploc	http://www.ziploc.com
Paul Arpin Van Lines	http://www.paularpin.com
Chef Boyardee	http://www.chefboy.com

As a reminder, here is a list of the seven positioning strategies described in the main text:

Positioning by …product attributes and benefits
…price/quality
…use or application
…product class
…product user
…competitor
…cultural symbols

Finally, do you think that any of the above Web advertisements represent a **repositioning** effort? If so, which one(s)? Explain.

Fortune Brands is an international corporation that specializes in establishing and maintaining **brand equity** for products in a wide variety of markets. Visit the Fortune Brands homepage and answer the following questions:

Fortune Brands   http://www.fortunebrands.com

Prepare a descriptive list of the branded products featured on this Website. How do these brand names communicate the intended positive attributes of each product and thus help position them in consumers' minds? How does the concept of brand equity apply to each product?

Finally, what would you say is the main purpose of the Fortune Brands Website? Explain your answer. Is this different from the focus of the separate and distinct Websites maintained for each branded product? If so, how?

Because Web-based services such as online catalogs and search engines are basically intangible (i.e., you can't actually touch them), you may not immediately realize that the concept of packaging can be applied to this medium. But adjust your perspective a bit and you'll see how the same concerns that go into the packaging of an item in your local supermarket must also be addressed when designing an interactive Website. For example, let's look at two of the most popular search engines:

Yahoo!   http://www.yahoo.com

Excite!   http://www.excite.com

Just as in the Duracell battery example (see p. 57), design factors such as size, shape, color, and lettering all contribute to appeal of these "packages" — i.e., what you see (and interact with) on your screen. With this in mind, write a brief comparison of the appearance and interactive design of these services in terms of their packaging appeal. Be sure to address issues such as overall aesthetics, complexity of layout, ease of navigation, conspicuousness of ad placement, and any other variables you deem important. In the final analysis, which search engine do you prefer?

Why is it important for Website designers to be keenly aware of packaging issues? That is, what aspects of this medium (and how it is used) make the "packaging" of a Website (especially its main page) crucial to its success? How does this compare to the packaging issues faced by producers of physically tangible goods like batteries or breakfast cereal?

Chapter 3: ORGANIZING FOR ADVERTISING AND PROMOTION: THE ROLE OF AD AGENCIES AND OTHER MARKETING COMMUNICATION ORGANIZATIONS

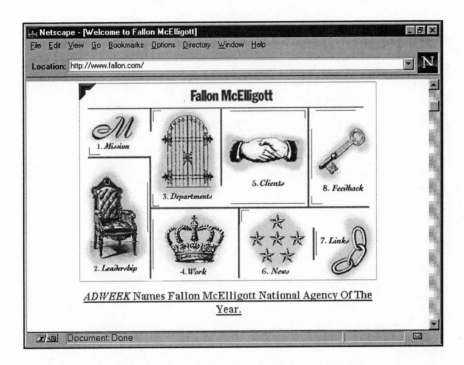

3-1   FALLON McELLIGOTT SHOWS BIG IS NOT ALWAYS BETTER   (65)

How do **advertising agencies** advertise themselves? To see what one hot agency is doing, take a look at the Fallon McElligott homepage:

> Fallon McElligott   http://www.fallon.com

As you read in the opening vignette for this chapter, Fallon is a mid-size company that's giving the larger ad agencies a run for their money. One reason for this is Fallon's exceptional strength in the area of account planning. See what you can find out about this aspect of Fallon's operation by perusing the above Website. How does Fallon sell its account planning services to potential **clients**? Write a brief summary of their account planning services and orientation. How does this orientation fit into the IMC framework?

(exercise continued on following page...)

Finally, compare Fallon's Website to one of the following large ad agency sites:

Leo Burnett Co.	http://www.leoburnett.com
J. Walter Thompson Co.	http://www.jwtworld.com
DDB Needham Worldwide	http://www.ddbn.com

What are the most significant differences between Fallon's site and the site you selected? If you were a major advertiser who could afford to hire any ad agency in the world, what would you consider to be the major advantages and disadvantages of choosing a large firm versus a mid-sized firm?

3-2   CENTRALIZED VS. DECENTRALIZED SYSTEMS OF ORGANIZATION   (68-72)

Which **organizational system** — **centralized** or **decentralized** — would you expect the following companies to use for their advertising and promotional activities? Justify your answer by citing definitions and concepts from the main text.

| General Mills, Inc. | http://www.generalmills.com |
| Jelly Belly | http://www.jellybelly.com |

3-3   IN-HOUSE AGENCIES   (72-4)

The welcome page for Fox World, one of many Websites maintained by the Fox Broadcasting Company, proudly proclaims that this site was "designed, produced and maintained by Fox in-house advertising." As you peruse Fox World, answer the questions below.

| Fox World | http://www.foxworld.com |

Why do you think that Fox chose to handle its advertising activities through an **in-house agency** rather than an outside firm? Given what you have learned about Fox's media marketing mix, why would an in-house agency be particularly advantageous for this company?

What would be the disadvantages for Fox if they chose to move these functions out-of-house? Would there be any advantages to this approach?

3-4   IMC PERSPECTIVE: BRAND MANAGERS TAKE THE WHEEL AT GM   (73)

As the authors point out in IMC Perspective 3-1, General Motors places heavy emphasis on creating strong and distinct brand identities not only for its major automobile lines (Chevrolet, Cadillac, Pontiac, etc.) but for the individual models that make up those lines. To see how **brand managers** are executing these strategies, take a look at the GM Website:

| General Motors | http://www.gm.com |

What is GM's positioning strategy for each major line? Between which brands would you expect to find the most overlap? What does GM hope to achieve by creating and maintaining these distinct identities?

Next, choose one major line within GM's product mix and visit the Website for that brand. Identify and describe the various models offered under this brand name. How would you characterize the strategy undertaken by this line's brand managers in terms of distinguishing between these models?

Finally, what are the potential benefits and pitfalls of creating wide variation among products sharing the same brand name?

3-5   TYPES OF ADVERTISING AGENCIES   (74-83)

Using any of the resources listed below, find one Website that corresponds to each of the three ad agency types described in the main text. That is, find one **full-service agency**, one **creative boutique**, and one **media buying service**.

Advertising World	http://advweb.cocomm.utexas.edu/world
Yahoo!	http://www.yahoo.com
Excite!	http://www.excite.com

Justify your choices by citing definitions and concepts from the book and relating them to the content on each site.

3-6   GAINING AND LOSING CLIENTS   (87-90)

This exercise provides us with our first look at the homepage for *Advertising Age*. Like the print version of this leading industry publication, the online edition of *Ad Age* contains a wealth of information and resources through which we can better explore the concepts and practices presented in the main text. We suggest you bookmark this site for future reference.

Advertising Age   http://www.adage.com

Locate the Daily Deadline section, which can be found under News & Features. This section contains condensed versions of top stories relating to the advertising industry.

Read all of the Daily Deadline articles for today — don't worry, there aren't that many, plus they're quite brief. Use these articles to illustrate and discuss some of the issues faced by ad agencies in terms of gaining and losing clients. How many of the issues and practices listed in the main text are relevant to the articles you read? Can you identify any other relevant factors depicted in these articles that are not mentioned in the textbook? If so, explain.

Using any of the resources listed below, find one Website that corresponds to each of the four **specialized marketing communications services** described in the main text. That is, find one **direct response agency**, one **sales promotion agency**, one **public relations firm**, and one **interactive agency**.

Advertising World	http://advWeb.cocomm.utexas.edu/world
Yahoo!	http://www.yahoo.com
Excite!	http://www.excite.com

Justify your choices by citing definitions and concepts from the book and relating them to the content on each site.

3-8   GLOBAL PERSPECTIVE: IMC NORTH OF THE BORDER   (91)

Marketing Magazine is Canada's only national weekly publication dedicated to the businesses of marketing, advertising and media. The Web-based version of this magazine is called Marketing Online, and it can be found at the following URL:

Marketing Online	http://www.marketingmag.ca

Marketing Online provides a wide array of current news, features, research reports, links, and other resources related to the advertising industry in Canada. Take a few moments to familiarize yourself with the structure and content of this site.

As the authors have done in Global Perspective 3-3, use an article or report from Marketing Online to illustrate one important and unique aspect of Canadian advertising vis-à-vis the United States. That is, identify and discuss one facet of Canada's business, media, or cultural environment that a U.S. advertiser should be aware of before entering the Canadian advertising arena.

You may want to start by looking for articles about U.S. companies which are trying to expand their markets north of the border. This site also has a search mechanism that could be of use in this exercise. Summarize the article you found and discuss the importance of this issue in terms of international marketing communications strategy.

3-9   INTERACTIVE AGENCIES   (93)

The online version of *Advertising and Marketing Review* features a regular column called "Advertising and the Internet" by Glen Morris. This column addresses some of the major challenges faced by interactive agencies and their advertisers. First, go to the *Advertising and Marketing Review* Website and locate the <u>Advertising and the Internet Archive</u>, which contains all of the columns written for this series since its inception in 1994.

Advertising and Marketing Review	http://www.ad-mkt-review.com

a) Choose one article from the archive that is of particular interest to you. Use this article to illuminate some of the unique issues faced by interactive agencies and their advertisers. That is, what does this article demonstrate about interactive technologies and how they differ from their traditional counterparts in terms of marketing communications?

b) What does this article demonstrate about the commonalities between interactive agencies and their traditional counterparts? That is, of all the marketing issues addressed in this article, which are equally applicable to interactive *and* non-interactive agencies and advertisers?

Chapter 4:   PERSPECTIVES ON CONSUMER BEHAVIOR

4-1   SATURN: A DIFFERENT KIND OF WEBSITE?   (101)

When General Motors launched its latest subsidiary line back in 1990, the world had never seen a car company quite like Saturn. But now that almost a decade has passed since the first Saturn rolled off the assembly line, can this company still set itself apart from the crowd? To see what Saturn is doing to maintain its unique image and operational strategy, take a look at its Website:

Saturn   http://www.saturn.com

Based on the features of this Website, how has Saturn continued to emphasize the six program philosophies listed in the chapter-opening vignette? That is, what evidence can you find for the following strategies: a new target market, partnering, sales training, no-dicker pricing, innovative advertising, and public relations? Cite specific examples whenever possible.

Are there any aspects of Saturn's current advertising strategy that surprised you? That is, has Saturn strayed at all from its original philosophy? If so, how?

Finally, what kind of challenges would you expect Saturn to face as it enters its second decade? How are these challenges different from those it faced early on?

4-2   SOURCES OF PROBLEM RECOGNITION   **(104-5)**

Demonstrate your understanding of the six sources of **problem recognition** by applying them to the primary product(s) advertised on the following homepages. Describe a likely scenario for each source: out of stock, dissatisfaction, new needs/wants, related products/purchases, marketer-induced problem recognition, and new products. Cite specific examples from each site wherever applicable.

Iams	http://www.iams.com
Orkin	http://www.orkin.com
Mindscape Games:	http://creatures.mindscape.com
Creatures	

What does the variation in your answers above demonstrate about the applicability of these factors to different types of products and services? Why is it important for marketers to appreciate this variation?

4-3   HIERARCHY OF NEEDS   **(106-8)**

Demonstrate your understanding of Maslow's **hierarchy of needs** by applying this theory to the primary product(s) advertised on the following Websites. That is, how do the five basic levels of human needs — physiological, safety, social/love & belonging, esteem, and self actualization — correspond to each product or service. Evaluate the applicability of each need level to these products/services.

Ithaca Gun	http://www.ithacagun.com
OraSure	http://www.orasure.com
Graceland	http://www.elvis-presley.com

Now that you have applied this theory to a few real-world situations, what is your evaluation of its usefulness in marketing communications? How well does Maslow's theory explain the motivation behind the consumption of these products? Stated another way, what are the limitations of this theory?

4-4   PERCEPTION   **(112-4)**

a)   The authors define **perception** as "the process by which an individual receives, selects, organizes, and interprets information to create a meaningful picture of the world." (p. 112) The three main aspects of this process are **sensation**, selecting information, and interpreting the information. Drawing from the definitions and discussions of these concepts in the main text, describe the perception process as it applies to your perusal of the following Website:

CareerPath.com	http://www.careerpath.com

Explore this multi-faceted process by examining your own experience of this Website. Consider your own needs and **motives** as you sense, select, and interpret the information on this site.

b) How do you think your perception would have differed if you had discovered this site on your own (i.e., in your personal job search) rather than as an academic exercise? What does this say about the relationship between motivation and perception?

4-5   BANNER ADVERTISING AND SELECTIVE PERCEPTION   (113-4)

Banner advertising is one of the most common advertising methods on the Web. You've probably seen hundreds of banners by now, but perhaps you don't know them by this name. Put simply, a banner is an advertisement (often a colorful picture or animated graphic) positioned prominently on a commercial site that provides an eye-catching and "click-able" link to an advertiser's company homepage. Banners are similar to magazine ads and highway billboards, but with one clear advantage: instant access! For example, if you company's banner pops up during a Yahoo! search session, all the user has to do is click on it and — voila! — they've made the jump to your Website.

CNN Interactive is one of many news Websites that feature banner advertising. Take a few moments to familiarize yourself with this remarkable service and answer the questions below.

CNN Interactive   http://www.cnn.com

a) How does the concept of **selective perception** apply to the banner advertising featured on this site? How can the four aspects of selective perception — **selective perception, selective attention, selective comprehension, and selective retention** — be used to explain the effectiveness of this kind of advertising? Which of these processes is the most critical for banner advertisers to recognize and overcome? Explain your answer.

b) Does selective perception apply differently to TV commercials than it does to Web banners? As you prepare your answer, consider the potential differences between TV "channel surfing" and "surfing the Web." Put another way, do people utilize and perceive CNN Interactive differently than the original CNN?

4-6   ALTERNATIVE EVALUATION   (114-7)

a) For the purpose of this exercise, imagine that you are researching an impending major purchase. This might be a new computer product (software, hardware, or peripheral), home appliance, automobile, audio/video component, or sporting good. Whatever product you choose, make sure it is one that is advertised on the Web by at least a few different manufacturers.

Walk yourself through the process of shopping around for this item on the Web. Search engines such as Yahoo! (www.yahoo.com) and Excite! (www.excite.com) will probably be of great value in your identification of brand alternatives. Follow this imaginary exercise through to a final (albeit mock) purchase decision.

(exercise continued on following page...)

Prepare a brief description of your research, evaluation, and decision process. What was your evoked set and how did you arrive at it? Did reminder advertising play a role in this process? What **evaluative criteria** did you consider as you approached your buying decision? What role did **functional** and/or **psychosocial consequences** play in your evaluation of alternatives?

b) Had this been an actual purchase decision, what other information sources would you have used? Would you have used the Web at all? What are the advantages and disadvantages of the Internet versus other information sources in terms of researching and evaluating product alternatives?

4-7   ATTITUDE CHANGE STRATEGIES   (118)

Identify and describe all of the attitude change strategies embodied in the following Websites. Cite specific examples whenever possible.

The Steel Alliance	http://www.thenewsteel.com
Gorton's	http://www.gortons.com
Kodak Picture Network	http://www.kodakpicturenetwork.com

4-8   THE PURCHASE DECISION AND BRAND LOYALTY   (119-20)

What are the following companies doing to promote **brand loyalty** via their Websites?

Burpee	http://garden.burpee.com
Digital Computer	http://www.digital.com
Smucker's	http://www.smucker.com

Evaluate the Web as a medium for instilling brand loyalty. What are its strengths and weaknesses in this area as compared to traditional marketing channels?

4-9   ENVIRONMENTAL INFLUENCES ON CONSUMER BEHAVIOR   (128-32)

a) Use the Levi's Website to illustrate the five environmental influences on **consumer behavior**: **culture**, **subculture**, **social class**, **reference groups**, and **situational determinants**.

Levi.com   http://www.levi.com

Discuss the potential impact of each environmental influence on the consumption of this company's products.

b) How do you think these factors have shaped Levi Strauss' advertising strategy? Does this Website place particular emphasis on one or more of these influences? If so, explain how while citing specific examples. Conversely, which environmental influences seem *least* relevant to the Web advertising for these products?

4-10   GLOBAL PERSPECTIVE: CULTURAL DIFFERENCES CHALLENGE   (129)
U.S. ADVERTISERS

McDonald's is one of the most universally recognized global advertisers. McDonald's success in so many foreign markets is due, in part, to its sensitivity to cultural differences. Check out the following Website to learn more about this aspect of McDonald's international marketing strategy:

McDonald's   http://www.mcdonalds.com

Once you've entered the main site, find the Around The World link. This will lead you to a World Tour of McDonald's franchises. As you complete the tour, take note of every case in which McDonald's has altered its standard marketing or operational formula in order to address cultural variation.

Can you think of any other cultural differences McDonald's might face in other foreign markets not featured on this Website? If so, describe them.

Chapter 5:   THE COMMUNICATION PROCESS

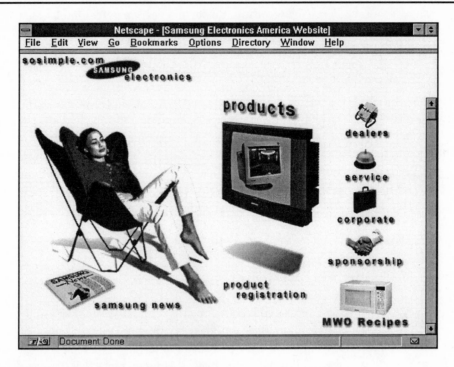

5-1   SAMSUNG REMAKES ITS IMAGE   (137)

As you read in the chapter-opening vignette, Samsung Electronics America (SEA) recently embarked on a major integrated marketing communications campaign designed to increase awareness of the company, improve its corporate image, and gain more acceptance of its products in North America. To see how Web advertising fits into this campaign, take a look at the SEA homepage:

        Samsung Electronics America   http://www.sosimple.com

a)   List and describe the ways in which SEA has used the Web to remake its image. Give examples of homepage elements that are consistent with the first series of new SEA magazine ads and TV commercials described in the vignette. Furthermore, how does this Website go *beyond* those print and broadcast ads to generate momentum for other aspects of the campaign? Discuss the advantages and disadvantages of television, print media, and the Web in terms of accomplishing the goals of SEA's aggressive re-marketing strategy.

b)   Next, take a look at the homepage for SEA's parent company in Korea:

        Samsung Electronics Co., LTD   http://www.sec.samsung.co.kr

Compare and contrast this Website with SEA's. What is the primary theme of each site? What do the differences between these sites say about the advertising challenges faced by corporations competing in a global marketplace?

5-2   A BASIC MODEL OF COMMUNICATION, PART 1   (138-45)

The authors have presented a basic model of **communication** comprised of six elements: **source encoding, message**, **channel**, **receiver/decoding**, **noise**, and **response/feedback**. Demonstrate your understanding of these concepts and processes by applying them to the following Website:

> Wendy's   http://www.wendys.com

In your discussion of these six elements, be sure to cite specific examples whenever possible. As you prepare your response, keep in mind the multifaceted nature of the above concepts and processes. For example, is there more than one message being transmitted here? Also, pay particular attention to the medium-specific variables that may shape the receiver's experience. That is, how does the Web user environment uniquely influence each aspect of the communication process?

5-3   A BASIC MODEL OF COMMUNICATION, PART 2   (138-45)

(*Note: In order to do this exercise, you must have already completed Exercise 5-2.*)

a)   Building on your response to Exercise 5-2, compare and contrast Web advertising with television advertising vis-à-vis the authors' basic model of communication. That is, how does a Wendy's TV commercial differ from the Wendy's Website in terms of source encoding, message, channel, receiver/decoding, noise, and response/feedback? How do these differences define the boundaries for what these forms of advertising can accomplish?

b) Repeat the above Exercise 5-3a, but this time compare and contrast Web advertising with print advertising (i.e., newspaper and magazine).

5-4   ANALYZING THE RECEIVER   (145-6)

a) For both of the following Websites, identify and describe all applicable levels of audience aggregation. Where possible, cite specific examples of marketing communication elements aimed at the following audience aggregation levels: individual and group audiences; niche markets; market segments; and mass markets and audiences.

> Dell Computer   http://www.dell.com
> Sallie Mae   http://www.salliemae.com

b)   Consider the following quote from the main text: "Unlike personal or face-to-face communications, mass communications do not offer the marketer an opportunity to explain or clarify the message to make it more effective." With this statement in mind, would you define the Web as a form of mass communication? Explain your answer. Further, does the Web afford advertisers the ability to communicate on the individual level of audience aggregation? If so, how?

Purchasing a discreet, tangible object is probably the most familiar consumer behavior one would associate with the advertising response process. For some Web-based businesses, however, product consumption is not measured in units sold. The creators of commercial search engines like Yahoo! simply want their free services to be used by as many people as possible, and as often as possible. The primary product — Web navigation assistance — is not bought, but rather utilized at no cost to the "consumer." Company income is generated primarily through the sale of banner ads (see Exercise 4-5) to be featured on the site. Attracting the maximum number of frequent users is important because the more exposure Yahoo! can guarantee potential advertisers (i.e., the more user "hits" they can promise), the more banner ads they will be able to sell *and* the more they can charge for these ads.

a)   Let's use this unique product adoption scenario to explore the four traditional response hierarchy models presented in the main text. To review, these are: 1) the **AIDA model**; 2) the **hierarchy of effects model**; 3) the **innovation adoption model**; and 4) the **information processing model**. First, choose one of the following search engine Websites as a basis for your response. To get the most out of this exercise, we suggest you select a site you are *not* already familiar with.

AltaVista	http://www.altavista.digital.com
Excite!	http://www.excite.com
Infoseek	http://www.infoseek.com
Lycos	http://www.lycos.com
Magellan	http://www.mckinley.com
Open Text	http://index.opentext.net
WebCrawler	http://www.webcrawler.com
Yahoo!	http://www.yahoo.com
ZD Net	http://www.zdnet.com

Use your chosen site to illustrate the four traditional response hierarchy models listed above, including their component stages. How do these models illuminate the process a prospective "consumer" (like you) might go through in considering this search engine for regular use? You may want to use Figure 5-3 (p. 147) as a framework for constructing your answer. Be sure to cite specific Website examples wherever possible.

b)   What difficulties (if any) did you encounter in applying these models to the search engine scenario? Do you think that these models are equally applicable to purchase and non-purchase situations? Explain.

5-6   GLOBAL PERSPECTIVE: CHANGING THE IMAGE OF AIR CANADA   (150)

a) As you read in Global Perspective 5-3, Air Canada hired a U.S. design firm in 1992 to develop a corporate identity that would sever its perceived ties to the Canadian government, which Canadians view as "stodgy, bureaucratic, and dull." A poll indicating that 49 percent of Canadians were "very dissatisfied" with their government provided further incentive for this marketing shift. To see how Air Canada is using the Web to promote its new image, check out the following Website:

Air Canada   http://www.aircanada.ca

Citing specific examples whenever possible, identify and describe all of the ways in which Air Canada's Website echoes the new marketing strategy discussed in the main text. In your opinion, are these aspects of the Website effective? Explain. Are there any potential pitfalls in this strategy?

b) Next, take a look at the Website for Air Canada's primary competitor, Canadian Airlines International:

Canadian Airlines Intl.   http://www.cdnair.ca

Compare and contrast these two companies in terms of the corporate identities they promote through these sites. What are the primary similarities and differences? Besides the obvious variables of price and flight availability, why do you think the flying public might choose one airline over the other? How does each company attempt to gain competitive advantage in these areas?

5-7   THE LOW-INVOLVEMENT HIERARCHY: TV vs. THE WEB   (151-3)

For the purposes of this exercise, choose a low-involvement product whose television advertising you are familiar with. You may want to choose a new product you've seen a TV commercial for in the past few days, or you might opt for a familiar product whose TV commercials you can recall from the recent past. Either way, the company behind this product must also advertise it via the Web. Using whatever Web navigation tools are necessary (e.g., search engines), locate the official homepage for your product. (The easiest thing to do, of course, is to choose a commercial that already contains a Website address.)

a) Identify your product and explain why you describe it as low-involvement. Also, be sure to give the URL (Website address) for its homepage so that your instructor(s) may peruse the site.

b) Use the **low-involvement hierarchy** to illuminate the advantages and disadvantages of using the Web to advertise this product. Your response should compare and contrast this Website with the TV commercial(s) you have seen in terms of viewer/user perception and exposure environment.

c) In general, how can Krugman's theory and the low-involvement hierarchy be applied to evaluating the potential effectiveness of Website advertising for low-involvement products? What are the inherent media-based limitations of both television and the Web in this area? What does the advertising for your chosen product demonstrate about how these two media can be used to complement each other?

Which of the four strategies that make up the FCB planning model can be most easily applied to the primary product(s) advertised on the following Websites? Explain your choice in each case.

Hallmark	http://www.hallmark.com
Aristokraft	http://www.aristokraft.com
LifeStyles	http://www.lifestyles.com
Newman's Own	http://www.newmansown.com

In what ways do these Websites reflect the possible implications (test, media, and creative) listed for each strategy in the FCB grid (Figure 5-8, p. 156)? Cite specific examples wherever possible.

Conversely, which homepage elements run counter to what you might expect if the Foote, Cone & Belding agency handled these marketing efforts? Specifically, do any of these sites promote products for which the FCB model probably would not prescribe Web advertising at all? Explain.

5-9   THE COGNITIVE RESPONSE APPROACH   (157-9)

First, obtain a recent issue of your favorite magazine. Next, select any full-page advertisement that is of interest to you, but make sure it includes a Website address for the featured product. Go to this Website and use its contents to discuss the **cognitive response** approach to the communication process. Give examples (both hypothetical and based on your own reactions) to illustrate the various responses that typify the three basic categories of this approach — product/message thoughts, source-oriented thoughts, and **ad-execution-related thoughts**.

Finally, compare this Website to the original magazine ad you selected. Looking at these two marketing efforts side by side, what role are medium-based differences likely to play in consumers' cognitive responses to these advertisements? That is, can similar ads for the same product generate different thought reactions solely because of differences in the mechanism of delivery? If so, which aspects of each medium are particularly useful for curtailing negative thoughts?

5-10   THE ELABORATION LIKELIHOOD MODEL (ELM)   (159-62)

One current marketing trend in the motion picture industry is the proliferation of individual Websites for major new release movies. To see this in action, check out the movie section of your local newspaper. (*Note: if your local paper doesn't carry space ads for first-run movies, then seek out a metropolitan newspaper in your region.*) For the purpose of this exercise, select one movie ad featuring a Website address. This ad should promote a new movie that you are immediately attracted to and would strongly consider seeing (but haven't yet). We will use this space ad and its corresponding Website to explore the **elaboration likelihood model (ELM)** of persuasion.

(*exercise continued on following page...*)

a) First, would you say that your movie choice was based on a low elaboration or high elaboration process? You answer should define both terms and explain why each does or doesn't apply to your initial selection process.

b) Next, peruse the Website for your chosen movie (be sure to include the URL in your answer). Compare and contrast this Website with its corresponding newspaper ad. Which **route to persuasion** — **central** or **peripheral** — would you associate with each advertising medium? Why? How would these concepts apply to a television commercial for the same movie? After exploring this Website, has your motivation to see this film changed in any way? Explain how and why using concepts from the ELM.

c) In general, what are the implications of the ELM for the motion picture industry? Specifically, what does the ELM illuminate about the relative strengths and weaknesses of newspaper ads, Websites, and TV commercials in terms of attracting paying audiences for new movies? What does your analysis say about the complementary relationships among these media?

d) Finally, which medium is most likely to motivate repeat customers (i.e., people who see the same movie more than once)? Explain your choice.

Chapter 6: SOURCE, MESSAGE, AND CHANNEL FACTORS

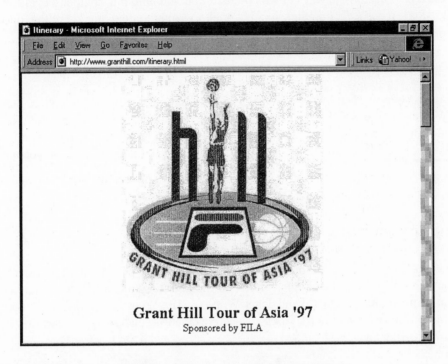

Grant Hill Tour of Asia '97
Sponsored by FILA

6-1 ENDORSEMENTS: WHERE NICE GUYS FINISH *FIRST* (165)

Grant Hill is one of many star athletes under contract with Fila for product endorsement. But in the fall of 1997, Hill set himself apart from the crowd by signing a new seven-year deal worth at least $80 million. The deal, one of the largest sports endorsement contracts ever, not only guarantees Hill a generous financial reward, but also makes him chairman of a committee that will advise Fila on selecting other athletes for endorsement contracts as well as on licensing deals involving Fila. [Source: *Rochester Democrat and Chronicle*, page D-2, 9/24/97.]

Fila features Hill not only on its corporate Website, but also on a separate site developed exclusively for the basketball superstar. These two sites can be found at the following URL's:

Fila	http://www.fila.com
Grant Hill	http://www.granthill.com

How does each of these Websites highlight Hill's "nice guy" or "nonabrasive, good-humored, All-American" image? Given what you read about Hill's image in the chapter-opening vignette, were there any aspects of these sites that surprised you? If so, explain.

Based on what you've learned, how would you characterize the relationship between Grant Hill and Fila? Does this arrangement go beyond the typical endorsement deals with which you are familiar? Besides financial rewards, what do Hill and Fila stand to gain, respectively, through this relationship? What potential pitfalls can you identify for both parties? Explain.

6-2   THE PERSUASION MATRIX   (166-7)

Use examples from the Newman's Own Website to demonstrate your understanding of the **persuasion matrix**. Discuss the ways in which this tool could help this company evaluate the following decisions: receiver/comprehension, channel/presentation, message/yielding, and source/attention.

Newman's Own   http://www.newmansown.com

Which central question implied by the persuasion matrix is most directly applicable to their decision to invest in Website advertising? Assuming that the use of Paul Newman's name and likeness is a primary reason for the success of these products, which matrix variable(s) is/are most relevant to this strategy? Finally, where does this company's charitable giving strategy fit into the persuasion matrix?

6-3   SOURCE FACTORS   (167-81)

Many major advertisers rely on high-profile celebrities to sell their products and services through television commercials. Current examples of this familiar strategy include Sprint (Candice Bergen) and American Express (Jerry Seinfeld and Tiger Woods). The Websites for these two companies, however, contain little or no mention of their respective celebrity endorsers. To see this for yourself, check out the following sites:

Sprint   http://www.sprint.com
American Express   http://www.americanexpress.com

What might account for the lack of celebrity endorsement content on these sites? As you formulate your response, consider the following questions:

What are the primary marketing objectives of these Websites?

How do these objectives differ from those of their corresponding TV commercials?

Finally, how might the various **source** factors discussed in this chapter explain why these companies chose not to use celebrities for their online advertisements and services?

6-4   USING CORPORATE LEADERS AS SPOKESPEOPLE   (171)

Though there are many potential advantages to using corporate leaders as spokespeople, this strategy can have its drawbacks. Just like celebrity endorsers, corporate leaders must be likeable, admirable, charming, and/or attractive in order to instill consumers with positive feelings about their products. Or maybe not…

Take a look at how Helmsley Hotels turned an apparent marketing disaster into a uniquely creative and successful advertising campaign. *Note: if you aren't familiar with the checkered history of this company's founder, we suggest you search* Yahoo! *for the keywords "Leona Helmsley."*

Helmsley Hotels   http://www.helmsleyhotels.com

What is the main theme of this campaign? What does this demonstrate about the limitations of likability and **attractiveness** as ways of measuring the advertising potential of celebrity endorsers and corporate spokespeople? What role does creativity (and in this case, humor) play in making the most of these personalities?

6-5   APPLYING LIKABILITY: USING CELEBRITIES   (174-7)

Unlike the companies featured in Exercise 6-3, Discover Card does not rely on one or two celebrity endorsers to promote their services. Instead, this company has enlisted the support of almost a dozen (possibly more by the time you read this) popular, albeit lesser-known, personalities. All of these endorsers are highlighted on the Discover Card Website:

Discover Card   http://www.discovercard.com

How might the factors discussed on pp. 174-7 account for Discover Card's multi-celebrity endorsement strategy? That is, how might you explain this company's decision to use a group of up-and-coming celebrities rather than building their entire campaign around a single mega-star? What are the potential advantages and disadvantages of these two endorsement strategies?

6-6   UNDERSTANDING THE MEANING OF CELEBRITY ENDORSERS   (177-9)

How can Grant McCracken's meaning transfer model be used to analyze the potential effectiveness of the following celebrity endorsement-based ad campaign?

"Milk, Where's Your Moustache?"   http://www.whymilk.com

How does the meaning transfer model illuminate this organization's decision to use many celebrity endorsers instead of just one?

6-7   IMC PERSPECTIVE: CHOOSING A CELEBRITY ENDORSER   (180)

According to the leading national media surveys, female celebrities have overtaken males in consumer appeal (see IMC Perspective 6-3 for more on this topic). Though the same probably cannot be said of female athletes compared to their male counterparts (yet), a similar trend can be seen in sports-related marketing. To see one real-world example of this, take a look at the Nike Website.

(exercise continued on following page...)

Nike   http://www.nike.com

Identify and describe the female athlete endorsements on this site. Compare and contrast these presentations with those featuring male athletes. Were there any major thematic differences between these presentations? If so, describe them. If not, what might account for this consistency?

Can you think of any trends in professional and/or amateur sports that might contribute to the increasing endorsement power of female athletes? Do you think that there will ever be a time when a female sports star will command the advertising attention now reserved for athletes like Michael Jordan and Tiger Woods?

6-8   MESSAGE STRUCTURE   (181-5)

Demonstrate your knowledge of message structure by applying the following concepts to the Website below: order of presentation, conclusion drawing, message sidedness, refutation, and verbal vs. visual message characteristics.

Democratic National Committee   http://www.democrats.org

As always, cite specific examples to support your answer. Furthermore, be sure to address the ways in which these structural elements are shaped by the unique interactive characteristics of the Web (as opposed to print and broadcast media).

6-9   MESSAGE APPEALS   (185-9)

Identify and describe the various message appeals used in the following Website advertisements:

Krank$_2$0   http://www.rocketcola.com
DIRECTV   http://www.directv.com
American Lung Association   http://www.lungusa.org

If any of these appeals do not fall within one of the three categories outlined in the main text (**comparative advertising, fear appeals, humor appeals**), how would you classify them? Did you find any instances of multiple appeal types for the same product, service, or idea? If so, why might you expect to find these multi-faceted campaigns on the Web as opposed to other media?

Find a magazine or newspaper advertisement that contains a corresponding Website. With your chosen print publication in hand, visit the specified URL and answer these questions:

Identify and describe the product, service, or idea you chose. In which print publication does this ad appear? Be sure to submit a copy of the print ad (original or photocopy) including the URL so that your instructor can access the corresponding Website.

Compare and contrast these two marketing pieces in terms of the following channel factors: difference in information processing, effects of context and environment, and effects of **clutter**.

What does your analysis indicate about the relative strengths and weaknesses of these two media for promoting this product/service/idea? Do you think this advertiser has effectively capitalized on these media-specific strengths while minimizing the respective weaknesses? If not, make specific suggestions for improvements in these areas.

Chapter 7:   ESTABLISHING OBJECTIVES & BUDGETING FOR THE PROMOTIONAL PROGRAM

TM © 1997 Kellogg Company

**7-1   CAN THE WEB HELP CEREAL COMPANIES *MILK* THEIR AD   (197)
DOLLARS TO AVOID AN INDUSTRY *CRUNCH*?**

As you read in the chapter-opening vignette, Thomas Knowlton, president of Kellogg's North America, says that with the recent cereal price cuts, "We can't afford advertising that isn't working. We are going to be more demanding with our brands, and only proven ad campaigns will get full funding." To see for yourself how the top three U.S. cereal companies — Kellogg's, General Mills, and Post — are using the Web to fortify their marketing mixes, take a look at the following Websites:

Kellogg's	http://www.kelloggs.com
General Mills	http://www.youruleschool.com *and* http://www.generalmills.com
Post Cereal	http://www.post100.com *and* http://www.kraftfoods.com

(exercise continued on following page...)

First, compare and contrast the various Web advertising strategies undertaken by each company. How would you describe the central theme(s) of each campaign? Which target market(s) does each company seem to cater to the most? Cite specific examples to support your answer.

Thinking back to what you learned in Chapter 5, would you say that breakfast cereal is a low- or high-involvement product? Explain. Given your answer to this question, discuss the strengths and weaknesses of the Web as a tool for driving demand for this product. When it comes to breakfast cereal, do you think the Web is better for attracting new customers or keeping old ones (i.e., promoting brand loyalty)? Why?

Finally, why might these companies emphasize Website marketing during periods of decreased advertising expenditures? Considering Knowlton's above statement, what do you think are the most significant challenges faced by Website advertisers in terms of assessing the success or failure of their online campaigns?

7-2 MARKETING VERSUS COMMUNICATIONS OBJECTIVES (200-1)

Though it is impossible to precisely determine an organization's **marketing** and **communications objectives** simply by examining its advertisements, we can nevertheless explore these critical concepts by looking at a few real-world examples.

Dirt Devil	http://www.dirtdevil.com
U.S. Navy Recruiting	http://www.navy.com
MADD	http://www.madd.org

What are your best guesses as to the marketing and communications objectives behind each of the above advertising campaigns? Cite specific examples to support your conjectures. Why is it important to differentiate between these two kinds of objectives?

7-3 PROBLEMS WITH SALES OBJECTIVES (202-3)

Although the Quaker State Corporation is best known for its line of motor oils and lubricants, this company is also a major supplier of consumer products and services to the automotive aftermarket. You will find the Quaker State Website at the following URL:

Quaker State   http://www.quakerstate.com

After acquainting yourself with this company and the major features of this site, follow the link for Consumer Offers and Promotions. Use examples from this collection to discuss and demonstrate the inherent problems with sales objectives outlined in the main text. Be sure to illustrate a possible **carryover effect** using one of Quaker State's consumer offers or promotions. Why is it important for advertisers to be aware of these problems and limitations?

7-4   IMC PERSPECTIVE: RELAUNCHING INFINITI   **(204)**

Picking up where IMC Perspective 7-1 left off, let's look at Infiniti's latest ad campaign:

Infiniti Motors   http://www.infinitimotors.com

How would you describe Infiniti's current marketing strategy? What is its central message? In what ways does this strategy resemble previous campaigns you read about on p. 204? How does it differ? Do you think that Infiniti has again reinvented its image?

7-5   COMMUNICATIONS EFFECTS PYRAMID   **(206-9)**

This exercise asks you to demonstrate your knowledge of the communications effects pyramid by applying this model to a recently launched product. First, you'll need a new product upon which to base your response. The *Windows Magazine* homepage provides us with a convenient connection to dozens of such items:

Windows Magazine   http://www.winmag.com

Look under the heading Latest News for a link labeled <u>New Products</u>. Here you will find reviews of some of the latest Windows-based utilities, desktop systems, Web applications, games, and educational items. What makes this collection especially useful is its inclusion of a source company Website URL for each product.

Choose one product and discuss how this company might use the communications effects pyramid to develop communications objectives for an advertising campaign. What stage do you think this product is in currently? What is the major focus of this stage? Looking at the Website for this company, what are the apparent communications objectives for this product right now? Finally, using Figures 7-3 and 7-4 as models, devise a series of overall objectives for each subsequent stage.

With regard to this product, at which stage of the communications effects pyramid is Website advertising least useful? Most useful? Which other media and promotional avenues do you think would be most effective at each stage?

7-6   FACTORS RELATED TO SUCCESS OF ADVERTISING FOR   **(207-10)**
**   NEW PRODUCTS**

One of the most famous rivalries in the computer software business is the ongoing battle between Microsoft and Netscape for domination in the Web browser market. Let's see which of these two giants does a better job of advertising its latest browser package by judging them according to the success factors listed in Figure 7-5.

(exercise continued on following page...)

| Microsoft | http://www.microsoft.com |
| Netscape | http://www.netscape.com |

First, locate the sections focusing on the latest versions of Internet Explorer (Microsoft) and Communicator (Netscape). These areas should be easy to find since these are flagship products for both companies. Next, assess each company's performance in the following areas:

- Communicating that something is different about the product
- Positioning the brand difference in relation to the product category
- Communicating that the product difference is beneficial to customers
- Supporting the idea that something about the product is different and/or beneficial to customers

Cite specific examples from both Websites to illustrate each of these factors. Which firm has done a better job in each area? What about overall? If you feel that these two campaigns are relatively even-matched, what other factors might account for their success or failure?

Finally, if you had to decide between these two browser packages, which one did/would you choose for personal use? What role did advertising play in your selection?

7-7   DAGMAR: AN APPROACH TO SETTING OBJECTIVES   (210-4)

The purpose of this exercise is to apply (or at least try to apply) one of the most traditional advertising strategy models to one of the *least* traditional campaigns ever devised by a major advertiser. What would Russell Colley, developer of the **DAGMAR** model, think of Benetton's revolutionary approach to image advertising? To find out more about Benetton's controversial marketing practices, take a look at their company Website:

Benetton   http://www.benetton.com

Follow the ADVERTISING link and you will see that Benetton has devoted a substantial portion of this site to showcasing and discussing its groundbreaking ads. We suggest you devote as much time as you can to viewing these ads and reading all of the supporting text. While these pieces do not represent the whole of Benetton's advertising efforts, for the purposes of this exercise you should only focus on this particular aspect of their marketing strategy.

How does Benetton's unique approach fit into Colley's hierarchical model of the communications process (if at all)? Can the four primary stages of this model — awareness, comprehension, conviction, and action — be applied here? If so, how? If not, why not?

Finally, considering what you read about this company's advertising philosophy and objectives, how do you think the marketing people at Benetton would react to the DAGMAR model? What does this say about the limitations of both the DAGMAR model and Benetton's radical objectives?

7-8   IMC PERSPECTIVE: SELLING HUSH PUPPIES TO A NEW GENERATION   (213)

To see how Wolverine Worldwide is using the Web to sell the classic Hush Puppies footwear line to a new generation of consumers, check out the following Website:

Hush Puppies   http://netpad.com/hushpuppies

What is the focus of this online campaign? Is this theme consistent with what you read in IMC Perspective 7-2? Do you think that the Web is an effective medium for reaching the intended audience for Hush Puppies? Why or why not?

Can you think of any improvements that might be made to this site? As you formulate your suggestions, keep in mind the target audience for this product as well as the key elements of past successful repositioning efforts.

7-9   SETTING OBJECTIVES FOR THE IMC PROGRAM   (214-7)

The main text highlights the San Diego Zoological Society as one organization that has been quite successful in its approach to setting objectives for the IMC program (see pp. 215-7). Using Figure 7-7 and the following Website for reference, answer the questions below:

San Diego Zoo   http://www.sandiegozoo.org

Though this organization has obviously made a significant investment in developing an outstanding Website, there is no mention of it in the tools/media section of Figure 7-7. How do you think Website marketing fits into the San Diego Zoological Society's objective-based promotional strategy? Discuss the different ways in which this site is being used — and could be used — to execute the various aspects of its IMC program. Be sure to address all areas included in Figure 7-7, including: advertising; sales promotions; public relations; cause marketing/corporate sponsorships/ events underwriting; direct marketing; and group sales.

Building on your response to these questions, discuss the critical link between setting objectives and selecting appropriate media for the various aspects of an IMC program.

7-10   TOP-DOWN VS. BUILD-UP APPROACHES TO BUDGETING   (222-32)

First, identify a specific product or product type that you know well and/or use regularly — perhaps one related to a hobby or recreational activity you enjoy. This product should be familiar and interesting to you. Though it is not a requirement for this exercise, it would help if you were familiar with the primary companies that compete for market share in this product category. Next, using one of the search engines below if necessary, locate the Website for one company that manufactures and/or sells this product (preferably one that you have done business with in the past):

(exercise continued on following page...)

Yahoo!	http://www.yahoo.com
Alta Vista	http://www.altavista.digital.com
Infoseek	http://www.infoseek.com

Using your prior knowledge of this product along with information from its corresponding Website, illustrate the overall differences between the **top-down** and **build-up approaches** to budgeting. Referring to Figure 7-12 as a model, devise a brief sketch of how these two basic strategies could be applied to establishing the advertising budget for this product.

Delving a bit further into this topic, demonstrate your knowledge of the following top-down methods by writing a brief description of how each could be used to establish the advertising budget for your chosen product/company: the **affordable method**, **arbitrary allocation**, **percentage-of-sales**, **competitive parity**, and **return on investment (ROI)**. In the case of competitive parity, which competitors might your chosen company use as benchmarks? How might they collect this information?

Finally, demonstrate you knowledge of the **objective and task method** (a build-up approach) by preparing a rough outline of how it might be applied to determining the advertising budget for your chosen product/company. (Refer to Figure 7-16 for guidance if necessary.) What are the main steps of this process?

Chapter 8: CREATIVE STRATEGY: PLANNING AND DEVELOPMENT

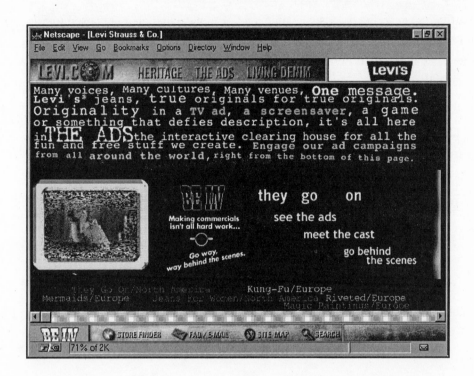

8-1 SELLING THE LEVI'S BRAND THROUGH IMAGE ADVERTISING   (239)

The Levi's Website provides us with a unique opportunity to explore this company's innovative approach to image-oriented advertising.

Levi.com   http://www.levi.com

After you have taken a few moments to acquaint yourself with the overall structure and features of this site, follow the link called <u>The Ads</u>. (*Note: By the time you read this, the name for this link may have changed slightly.*) This will lead you to a collection of Levi's ad campaigns aimed at North American and European audiences. Prepare a list of these ads and take note of which continent each ad is intended for.

Explore each of these ads as fully as you can. Go <u>Behind The Scenes</u> by following the appropriate links. In order to examine all of the ad-related resources on this site (i.e., video, audio, and animation), certain browser plug-ins may be required. Don't worry if your computer system doesn't have all of them. You can still complete this exercise using only the basic graphics and accompanying text provided for each ad.

(exercise continued on following page...)

a) For each featured ad, answer the following questions:

What is the main theme?

What kind of emotion or mood does it provoke?

Would you say that this ad has an "attitude"? If so, describe it.

Identify and describe the visual, sonic, and/or plot-related elements used to create this atmosphere.

What type of image is being portrayed here?

How is this image associated with the product?

b) Considering your responses to the above questions, did you notice any major thematic differences between the North American ads and their European counterparts? Summarize any patterns or trends you observed, citing specific examples whenever possible.

8-2   CREATIVE STRATEGY VS. CREATIVE TACTICS   (240)

Use examples from the following Website to demonstrate the difference between **creative strategy** and **creative tactics**.

Joe Boxer   http://www.joeboxer.com

Which aspects of this site are most directly shaped by creative strategy? How do these differ from those aspects reflecting the creative tactics chosen by this company? Why is it important for advertisers to distinguish between these two concepts?

8-3   THE IMPORTANCE OF CREATIVITY IN ADVERTISING   (241-3)

The authors have demonstrated the importance of creativity in advertising by focusing on Burger King's ever-changing campaign themes. To see what this fast food giant is doing to maintain its strong identity, let's visit the Burger King Website:

Burger King   http://www.burgerking.com

First, follow the Current Promotions link to see some of Burger King's latest promotions along with a current TV commercial. Has Burger King stuck with the "Get Your Burger's Worth" campaign adopted in 1994?

If so ➜ How does this Website reinforce the main theme of this campaign? Have any older themes (see Fig. 8-1) been integrated into the "Get You Burger's Worth" strategy? If so, identify them and discuss some possible reasons for the re-emergence of these themes.

If not ➜ What is the new theme and how does it differ from its predecessor? What is your best guess as to the reason for this change in creative strategy?

8-4　DIFFERENT PERSPECTIVES ON ADVERTISING CREATIVITY　(244-6)

As you read on page 244, "**advertising creativity** is the ability to generate fresh, unique, and appropriate ideas that can be used as solutions to communications problems. To be *appropriate* and effective, a creative idea must be relevant to the target audience." Furthermore, some would argue that when it comes to an advertising campaign, "it's not creative unless it sells." Let's use the Jolt Cola Website as a backdrop for our discussion of these perspectives.

Jolt Cola (Wet Planet Beverages)　　http://www.joltcola.com

Once you have accessed the above URL, click on the Jolt Cola logo. Take a few moments to explore this unique site. Chances are you've never seen anything quite like it. But is it effective advertising?

First, answer this question based solely on your gut feelings. All academic considerations aside, do you think this ad *works*? In your view, does this Website represent advertising creativity as defined above?

Next, answer this question according to the two extreme perspectives discussed at the top of p. 244.

Finally, assess the creative quality of the Jolt Cola Website according to the D'Arcy, Masius Benton & Bowles universal advertising standards. Use Figure 8-2 as a framework for constructing your assessment. Once your assessment is complete, discuss the limitations of using only these nine principles to judge the "quality" of an advertisement.

8-5　IMC PERSPECTIVE: GETTING EVERYONE INVOLVED IN　(246)
　　　　CREATIVE STRATEGY

As you read in IMC Perspective 8-2, the TBWA Advertising campaign for Absolut Vodka was designed to build awareness of the brand and make Absolut "a fashionable symbol of smartness and sophistication that consumers would want to be associated with." To see how this strategy has been translated into Web marketing, visit the Absolut site below:

Absolut Vodka　　http://www.absolutvodka.com

As you can see, "Absolut Kelley" has been replaced by a different media-inspired creative effort. Identify and describe the current installment in this ongoing series. How does this kind of Website content promote the advertising objectives described above? Would you even call this Website an "ad"? Why or why not? Finally, are there any potential pitfalls to this arguably indirect strategy?

8-6   INPUTS TO THE CREATIVE PROCESS   (177-9)

For the purpose of this exercise, find the Website for a specific branded product you use regularly. The following list of product classes may help you think of an appropriate choice: sporting goods, computer hardware/software, consumer electronics, automotive products, apparel, food items, health and beauty aids, etc. Just make sure that you select a product in which you have a personal investment as a brand-loyal user.

Imagine that you have been appointed to lead the creative team assigned to revamp the Website advertising for this product. Drawing on both your personal experience with this product and what you've learned about it online, describe the informal and formal background research you might undertake as you begin this creative process. Your description should be as specific as possible. Be sure to address the following topics in your discussion: informal fact-finding, **general preplanning input**, **product/service-specific research**, **problem detection**, **qualitative research input**, and **focus groups**. How can each of these inputs help you prepare for this undertaking?

8-7   IMC PERSPECTIVE: UNDERSTANDING HOW PEOPLE REALLY DRINK   (180)
MILK LEADS TO A CREATIVE ADVERTISING CAMPAIGN

Picking up where IMC Perspective 8-3 left off, let's visit the "got milk?" homepage to see how this campaign is being carried out via the Web:

                    "got milk?"   http://www.got-milk.com

Identify and describe the central theme(s) of this Website. Is the primary focus of this site the same as that of the "got milk?" ads described on p. 254?

> If so ➜ Do you think that the Web is a potentially effective medium for carrying out this campaign? Why or why not? Discuss the strategic advantages and disadvantages of the various media (online, print, broadcast, and outdoor) as venues for these kinds of persuasive messages.

> If not ➜ Why do you think a different approach was taken in applying this campaign to the Internet? What is the apparent target audience for this Website? Is this different from the target audience for the "got milk" TV ads? If so, how? How might you characterize the creative strategies behind these contrasting marketing efforts? How have these strategies influenced the creative tactics used to carry them out?

8-8   ADVERTISING CAMPAIGNS   (256-7)

Figure 8-4 lists some of the more enduring **general preplanning input** themes used by a variety of major corporations. To see how (and if) these themes have endured, check out the following Websites:

Nike	http://www.nike.com
Allstate Insurance	http://www.allstate.com
Hallmark Cards	http://www.hallmark.com
United Airlines	http://www.ual.com
BMW	http://www.bmwusa.com
State Farm Insurance	http://www.statefarm.com
Timex	http://www.timex.com

For each company Website, answer the following questions:

What campaign theme did you find? Is it the same theme listed in Figure 8-4?

If so ➔ How is this theme reinforced throughout this Website?

If not ➔ Has the old theme been modified, or has it been replaced altogether? In either case, how do you account for this change? How does the new theme differ from its predecessor?

Finally, if you couldn't identify a central campaign theme on any of these sites, why do you think the advertiser(s) in question chose not to integrate their well-known theme(s) into their online marketing?

8-9   THE MAJOR SELLING IDEA, PART 1   (257-62)

Exercise 8-3 asked you to consider the creative aspects of Burger King's current ad campaign. This time you will be looking at some of Burger King's primary competitors:

Taco Bell	http://www.tacobell.com
Subway	http://www.subway.com
Kentucky Fried Chicken	http://www.kentuckyfriedchicken.com
McDonald's	http://www.mcdonalds.com

Identify and describe the **major selling idea** behind each of the above advertising campaigns. Did the volume and variety of information, graphics, activities, and other features on these sites obscure any of these the major selling ideas? That is, did clutter get in the way of transmitting the big idea? If so, discuss the message transmission issues that Website marketers must be aware of when applying creative strategy to the online environment.

Next, compare and contrast the major selling ideas you identified. Be sure to note any thematic overlap between these campaigns.

Finally, if you couldn't identify a major selling idea in any of the above campaigns, why might this be a significant stumbling block for the advertiser(s) in question?

MCI Communications is one of a growing number of companies featuring television commercials on their Websites. MCI can be found at the following URL:

MCI   http://www.mci.com

To view this company's latest commercials, follow the <u>Connections</u> link and click on <u>MCI TV Ad Clips</u>. View all of these commercials and answer the following questions.

Is there a single major selling idea shared by all of these ads? If so, what is it?

Which of the following approaches best describes the basic creative strategy behind each of these ads? As always, cite specific examples to support your answer.

- Using a **unique selling proposition (USP)**
- Creating a brand **image**
- Finding the **inherent drama**
- Positioning

If you found a variety of approaches within this collection of commercials, do you think that this diversity might adversely affect MCI's reinforcement of the major selling idea? Or do you think that a multi-faceted TV campaign can be effective for promoting a single major selling idea? Explain.

If you found a single approach shared among all of these commercials, evaluate MCI's success (or failure) in carrying out this objective.

Chapter 9: CREATIVE STRATEGY: IMPLEMENTATION AND EVALUATION

9-1   CHEVY TRUCKS WEBSITE REINFORCES AN AMERICAN THEME   (265)

As you read in the chapter-opening vignette, one of the factors that convinced Bob Seger to allow his song, "Like a Rock," to be used in TV commercials for Chevy Trucks was the strong theme of American pride running through the proposed ad campaign. At that time, the American automobile industry was reeling from a surge in foreign car and truck sales in the U.S. As Seger put it, "There was this feeling that the Japanese were running us off our heels and maybe we could help."

That was almost a decade ago, and even though U.S. manufacturers have reclaimed a significant share of the overall automotive market, Chevy Trucks has continued to reinforce an American pride theme in its advertising program. To see this in action, take a look at the Chevy Trucks Website:

Chevy Trucks   http://www.chevrolet.com/truck/index.htm

Identify and describe all of the American cultural pride elements featured on this site. Be sure to cite specific examples of images, partnerships, endorsements, and supporting text used to bolster this theme.

Though American pride is still a significant thematic element within the Chevy Trucks creative strategy, their current areas of primary emphasis are *dependability*, *long-lasting quality*, and *meeting customer needs*. How is Chevy using their Website to reinforce these key messages?

Identify and describe the **advertising appeals** used on the following Websites. Cite examples to support your answer. Be sure to indicate whether each appeal is informational/rational or emotional. For each **informational/rational appeal** you find, indicate which of the following categories it falls into: feature, competitive advantage, favorable price, news, or product/service popularity appeal. For each **emotional appeal**, which personal or social-based feeling(s) is it based on (see Fig. 9-1)?

Milk-Bone	http://www.milkbone.com
Kidde Fire Protection	http://www.kidde.com
Nicorette	http://www.nicorette.com
Make-A-Wish Foundation	http://www.wish.org

Did you find any instances of combined appeals? If so, describe how these approaches are used to complement one another in each case. In your opinion, are these combinations appropriate and effective? Explain.

9-3   ADVERTISING APPEALS, PART 2   (266-74)

Exercise 9-2 asked you to consider the appeals used by a variety of advertisers. This time you are asked to compare and contrast the appeals from three closely related advertisers: branches of the U.S. armed forces. Specifically, identify and describe the appeals used by the U.S. Air Force, Army, and Navy to attract new recruits.

U.S. Air Force	http://www.airforce.com
U.S. Army	http://www.goarmy.com
U.S. Navy	http://www.navy.com

As above, be sure to indicate whether each appeal element is informational/rational or emotional. For each informational/rational appeal you find, indicate which of the following categories (if any) it falls into: feature, competitive advantage, favorable price, news, or product/service popularity appeal. For each emotional appeal you find, which personal or social-based feeling(s) is it based on (see Fig. 9-1)?

Did you find any instances of combined appeals? If so, describe how these approaches are used to complement one another in each case. In your opinion, are these combinations appropriate and effective? Explain.

Finally, compare and contrast these three Websites in terms of their advertising appeals. What are the most significant similarities and differences? Would you call these three organizations competitors of one another? If so, what kinds of appeals are used by each armed force to distinguish itself from the other two? Which appeal type seems most effective for this purpose? Explain.

9-4   IMC PERSPECTIVE: THE VACATION YOU TAKE IN YOUR MIND   (270)

To see how (and if) Norwegian Cruise Lines' "It's different out here" campaign is being carried out on the Web, visit the NCL site below and answer the questions that follow:

Norwegian Cruise Line   http://www.ncl.com

How is this Website an extension of the NCL marketing strategy described in IMC Perspective 9-1? Identify and describe the different appeals that make up this advertising effort. Compared to television and print ads, which appeal types is the Web particularly well suited to? Has NCL made the most of these strengths? If so, how?

Finally, let's look at how some of NCL's primary rivals are trying to distinguish themselves in this highly competitive market:

Carnival Cruise Lines   http://www.carnival.com
Celebrity Cruises   http://www.celebrity-cruises.com
Cunard Line   http://www.cunardline.com
Holland America Line   http://www.hollandamerica.com

For each competing cruise line, describe it's answer to NCL's "It's different out here" campaign. That is, identify the emotional appeals used by these companies to entice new customers. Compare and contrast these approaches in terms of the personal and social-based feelings (see Fig. 9-1) they are intended to exploit.

9-5   COMBINING RATIONAL AND EMOTIONAL APPEALS   (271-2)

In the fall of 1997, MasterCard announced that McCann-Erickson Worldwide would be charged with the creative development and execution responsibilities for all of its U.S. advertising in support of strengthening MasterCard's global payment brands. "We're confident that McCann-Erickson will help us effectively and consistently convey our vision in a way that differentiates MasterCard from its competition, and is relevant to consumers," said Nick Utton, senior vice president, U.S. Marketing. MasterCard's new advertising was set to debut by the end of 1997.

How might McCann-Erickson's emotional bonding technique help this agency execute a more effective ad campaign for MasterCard? Use Figure 9-2 as a guide for your critical discussion of the emotional appeals featured on the MasterCard Website:

MasterCard   http://www.mastercard.com

What is the ultimate goal of the emotional bonding technique? Why is this especially relevant to a financial services company like MasterCard?

Identify and describe the **creative execution styles** used in the following Website advertisements.

RotoRooter	http://www.rotorooter.com
Ginsana	http://www.ginsana.com
Volkswagen	http://www.vw.com
Dr. Seuss	http://www.randomhouse.com/seussville

Cite examples to support your answer, and be sure to indicate which of the following presentation formats each identified appeal/message represents:

Straight sell or factual message	Animation
Scientific/technical evidence	Personality symbol
Demonstration	Fantasy
Comparison	Dramatization
Testimonial	Humor
Slice of life	Combinations

9-7   CREATIVE TACTICS FOR PRINT ADS   (282-6)

First, obtain a recent issue of your favorite popular magazine. Next, select any full-page advertisement that is of interest to you, but make sure it includes a Website address for the featured product or service. Prepare a critical analysis of your chosen magazine ad in terms of the three basic print ad components discussed on pp. 282-6. That is, describe the **headlines**, **body copy**, and visual elements of this ad and discuss how the **layout** brings it all together.

Specifically, what is the headline and what is its function? Do you think this headline is effective? Why or why not? Is it a **direct** or **indirect headline**? Identify any accompanying **subheads** and summarize their purpose.

What kind of appeal(s) did you find in the body copy? Would you describe the appeal(s) as emotional or rational? Again, do you think this approach effective? Why or why not? If not, how could it be improved?

Discuss the visual elements of this ad. How do these reinforce the central appeal/message? Once again, do you think this approach is effective? Why or why not?

Finally, compare and contrast this print ad with its corresponding Website in terms of the above components. Can you think of any other components that need to be addressed when determining the creative tactics for a Website ad? What does this say about the key differences between print advertising and Website advertising?

9-8   CREATIVE TACTICS FOR TELEVISION   (286-90)

The Gap is one of a growing number of companies featuring television commercials on their Websites. Access the following URL and follow the instructions below to see the latest GapKids TV commercial.

The Gap   http://www.gap.com

Follow the <u>advertising</u> link and click on <u>GapKids television</u> to see a list of the available commercials for this highly successful line of children's clothing. Choose one of these TV spots and write a critical analysis according to the components discussed on pp. 286-90.

Specifically, what are the primary video elements and what is their function? How are they used to convey this commercial's central idea, message, or image? Next, describe the audio portion of this commercial. What roles do the spoken word, music, and/or other sonic elements play in reinforcing the appeal? Be sure to identify and describe any **voiceovers** or **jingles** used in this ad.

Finally, what is the apparent target audience for this commercial? Is there more than one? Explain. With this in mind, what is your assessment of this commercial's potential success?

9-9   IMC PERSPECTIVE: IS THE COMPANY THAT CHANGED   (291)
ADVERTISING STILL ON THE CUTTING EDGE?

Though Apple Computer's "1984" television commercial pushed the advertising envelope and helped Apple exceed its ambitious sales goal for the launch of its Macintosh line, this company has suffered a significant loss of market share in recent years to a growing number of IBM-compatible PC manufacturers. So while the Macintosh may have transformed personal computing forever, Apple seems to be having trouble keeping up with the very revolution it started.

To see how Apple is using television advertising in an attempt to reverse this trend, access their company Website:

Apple Computer   http://www.apple.com

As you can see, Apple has devoted a significant portion of this Website to the various media used to execute their current ad campaign. Follow the appropriate links to view the most recent Apple TV commercial and read more about the philosophy behind this campaign.

First, what is the major selling idea behind this ad campaign? Describe the nature of this appeal and the creative strategy behind it. Next, using Exercise 9-8 as a guide, write a critical analysis of this commercial according to the components discussed on pp. 286-90.

Finally, compare and contrast this campaign with the one described in IMC Perspective 9-4. How has Apple's "comeback" position influenced the creative strategy behind the current campaign?

(*Note: In order to do this exercise, you must have already completed Exercise 9-9.*)

Building on your response to Exercise 9-9, assess the current Apple television commercial according to the criteria for evaluating creative output discussed on pp. 292-4. In order to answer the seven questions that make up this evaluation, you will need to read all available information on the Apple Website regarding their current marketing and advertising objectives.

Chapter 10:   MEDIA PLANNING AND STRATEGY

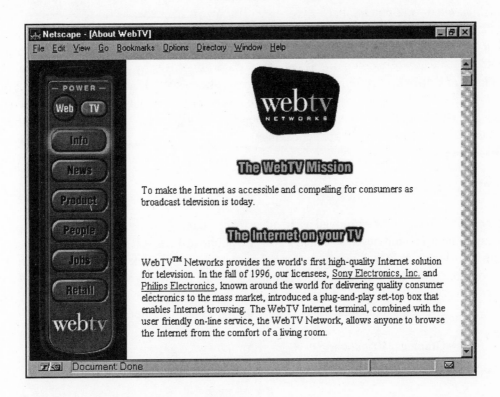

10-1   INTERACTIVE TV: BOOM OR BUST?   (297)

As you read in the chapter-opening vignette, the jury is still out on the future of interactive
television. Will "Internet TV" be the breakthrough that brings interactive television into the
mainstream? These three companies are counting on it:

WebTV	http://www.webtv.com
PC-TV	http://www.pctv.com
Enhanced TV (Oracle)	http://nc.oracle.com/html/home/index.htm

Compare and contrast these "Internet TV" initiatives. What are their similarities and differences?
Would you describe these companies as competitors, or do they represent complementary
technologies and/or services?

Given consumers' past resistance to interactive television, what are the unique advertising
challenges faced by these new media companies? That is, what are the key differences between
Oracle's marketing of Enhanced TV and, for example, Sony's introduction of a new television set
model based on traditional and accepted technology?

10-2   MEDIA PLANNING: SOME BASIC TERMS AND CONCEPTS   **(298-9)**

Use the following Website to demonstrate your knowledge of the following terms: **medium, media vehicle, reach, coverage,** and **frequency.** How do these terms apply to this site's purpose, delivery mechanism, content, and potential effectiveness?

The Rock & Roll Hall of Fame   http://www.rockhall.com

Did you have any difficulty applying these terms to the above site? If so, why do you think this was the case? Discuss the key conceptual differences between print, broadcast, outdoor, and Website advertising in terms of reach, coverage, and frequency. What do these differences imply about the limitations of advertising a given product exclusively via the Web?

10-3   PROBLEMS IN MEDIA PLANNING   **(299-302)**

Ever since the Web was first employed as an advertising channel, marketing and media experts have been trying to measure and describe exactly how the public utilizes this medium. Even basic questions like "how many Web users are there?" pose significant problems for researchers. To see how two organizations are taking up this challenge, visit the following Websites:

Nielsen Media Research   http://www.nielsenmedia.com

Graphics, Visualization   http://www.cc.gatech.edu/gvu/
and Usability Center   Click on WWW User Survey

Using these sites for reference, what are the major problems in **media planning** for Website advertisers vis-à-vis Web usage measurement? For each problem you identify, which of the following categories does it fall into: insufficient information, inconsistent terminologies, time pressures, or difficulty measuring effectiveness? Are any of these problems shared by other media? If so, explain.

10-4   IMC PERSPECTIVE: MEDIA SERVICES COMPANIES UNDER ATTACK   (301)

To see how Mediamark Research, Inc (MRI) is responding to criticisms like those discussed in IMC Perspective 10-1, take a look at their company Website:

Mediamark Research, Inc.   http://www.mediamark.com

Find and read all the information you can about MRI's print media readership research. If you have trouble finding relevant material, this site's SEARCH link might help. You should also scan MRI's press releases for company reactions to recent attacks. Identify and describe the most recent criticisms of MRI. Has this company changed any of its policies or methodologies in reaction to these attacks? What statements have they made in their own defense? In general, what are they doing to improve their research methods and, thus, the accuracy and relevance of their findings?

10-5   TARGET MARKET COVERAGE (309)

All of the leading search engine Websites give advertisers a way to focus their marketing efforts by linking user input to banner output (see Exercise 4-5 for more on banners). That is, these sites display different advertising banners depending on which keywords a user submits. For a demonstration of this process, go to Yahoo! (http://www.yahoo.com) and perform a series of searches using a variety of keywords. For the purposes of this exercise, keep your keywords fairly general — e.g., "baseball" rather than "Cal Ripken". Don't worry about the search results. Instead, pay attention to the banner ads that appear.

a)   Try keywords such as *fashion, insurance, construction*, and *music*. Do different keywords trigger different banners? If so, what patterns can you identify? What strategic advantage does this represent for Yahoo! advertisers?

b) If your company chose to advertise on Yahoo!, which keywords would you want linked to your banner? Make a keyword list for each of the following business types:

- Accounting software manufacturer
- Home video rental outlet
- Travel agency
- Women's sportswear retailer

c) Though different keywords will trigger different banners once a search has been initiated, the very first banner a user sees upon accessing Yahoo!'s main page is generated randomly. Discuss the ramifications of this variation in terms of target market coverage for Yahoo! advertisers.

10-6   SCHEDULING (310-1)

In developing and implementing their **media strategies**, why is scheduling a key issue for the following companies?

Secure Tax	http://www.securetax.com
Butterball	http://www.butterball.com
Claritin	http://www.allergy-relief.com

Which scheduling method — **continuity**, **flighting**, or **pulsing** — would you expect each company to use in promoting their products or services? Explain your choice.

10-7   REACH VS. FREQUENCY (311-3)

The main text uses examples from television advertising to illustrate the differences between reach and frequency as well as the key media planning issues surrounding these measures. Demonstrate your understanding of these two concepts by applying them to the following Websites:

(exercise continued on following page...)

ESPN SportsZone   http://espn.sportszone.com
CNN/SI   http://www.cnnsi.com

Let's say your company has arranged for the same banner ad to run at identical exposure rates on both sites. How do the concepts of reach and frequency apply to your ad's potential for being viewed by users of these sites? How might the terms **unduplicated reach** and **duplicated reach** apply to this situation?

How does this scenario compare to the television examples discussed in the main text? What does this demonstrate about the relative advantages and disadvantages of these advertising media?

10-8   MOOD   (316-8)

Certain media enhance the creativity of a message because they create a mood that carries over to the communication. What different mood-based images might be created for your product if you advertised it on the following Websites?

Car and Driver   http://www.caranddriver.com
Martha Stewart Living   http://www.marthastweart.com
Mother Jones   http://www.mojones.com
Fathering Magazine   http://www.fathermag.com

What kinds of advertisers did you find on each site? Did any of these surprise you? If so, explain.

10-9   FLEXIBILITY   (319)

The McDonald's Website takes full advantage of the interactive adaptability of this medium by offering two different "paths" a user can take depending upon the target market he or she represents. Check out both paths as you peruse the McDonald's site below:

McDonald's   http://www.mcdonalds.com

Identify and describe these two paths. How has McDonald's tailored the content of this site to achieve its marketing objectives for these two target audiences? What unique advantage of Website advertising does this demonstrate? As you answer this question, think about the limitations of a 30-second TV commercial or one-page print ad.

Which of the four flexibility scenarios (see p. 319, top) does this strategy address? In general, which scenario is most relevant to advertisers who rely heavily upon Website advertising to promote their products?

In their discussion of the relative costs of media, the authors have outlined the most common formulas used to determine magazine, newspaper, and television advertising rates. To see how Web banner advertising rates compare to the above standards, take a look at the homepages below and follow the specified links:

Open Text Index	http://index.opentext.net Click on Advertise Here
BizWeb	http://www.bizweb.com Click on Banner Ad Rates
Windows95.com	http://www.windows95.com Click on Advertising Info, then Advertising Prices

In addition, the following URL's will lead you to background information and definitions of terms that will help you understand the above rates.

> http://www.sjmercury.com/help/advertise.htm
> http://www.wilsonweb.com/wmt/issue16.htm
> http://www.win95mag.com/12_96/html/ad_definitions.html

Using all of the above resources, develop a formula representing the typical pricing structure for banner advertising. Be sure to define all of the terms within your formula.

Compare and contrast this formula with the following pricing standards: **cost per thousand, cost per ratings point**, and **daily inch rate**. Would you say that Web banner exposure opportunities are sold more like print ad space or television time? Explain.

Chapter 11: EVALUATION OF BROADCAST MEDIA

11-1   BOOM IN SPORTS PROGRAMMING SPILLS OVER TO THE WEB   (339)

For fans who just can't get enough of their favorite sports on TV, the ESPN SportsZone Website provides news, statistics, features, and a wealth of other resources and activities online, twenty-four hours a day. See this popular site for yourself at the following URL:

ESPN SportsZone   http://ESPN.SportsZone.com

a)   In what ways does this service go beyond the sports news and events coverage you'd find on ESPN's cable TV and radio networks? Specifically, which of these elements can *only* be executed via the Web? How do these Web-only features generate interest in ESPN's other services (if at all)? Which of these features are connected to sponsor product promotions? Discuss the strategic advantages of this kind of integrated marketing for both ESPN and its sponsors.

b)   Next, take a look at one of ESPN's primary cable *and* online competitors, CNN/SI:

CNN/SI   http://www.cnnsi.com

What are the major differences between the ESPN and CNN/SI sites? Why might people choose one over the other? If you're a sports fan, which site would you be more likely to visit on a regular basis? Why?

11-2   ADVANTAGES OF TELEVISION   (340-3)

This exercise requires you to identify a major corporation that uses both television commercials and Website advertising in its media mix. The easiest way to do this is to watch some prime-time network TV (i.e., ABC, NBC, CBS, or FOX). Since Website URL's are now a common feature of high-profile TV commercials, it shouldn't take long for you find an appropriate company. Once you've chosen a particular advertiser's commercial, be sure to take note of the time it ran and the program during which it appeared. Write a brief description of your chosen commercial, including its central theme and apparent target audience.

Next, access the specified URL. Use the content of this Website along with your notes about its corresponding TV commercial to discuss the relative advantages and disadvantages of these media for advertising this company's products and/or services. Organize your discussion in terms of the following categories:

- creativity and impact

- coverage and cost effectiveness

- captivity and attention

- selectivity and flexibility

As always, cite specific examples to support your analysis.

11-3   NETWORK TV: SELECTIVITY AND FLEXIBILITY   (342-3)

As you read on p. 342, network television has been criticized for being a nonselective medium, since it is difficult to reach a precisely defined market segment using TV advertising. But some selectivity is possible due to variations in the composition of audiences as a result of program content, broadcast time, and geographic coverage. With this in mind, discuss how advertisers might use the following network TV programs to reach different target audiences.

General Hospital	http://www.port-charles.com/gh
Goosebumps	http://www.foxkids.com/goose.htm
Monday Night Football	http://www.abcmnf.com
Today	http://www.msnbc.com/news/TODAY_front.asp

Specifically, what kinds of products might you expect to see advertised during these shows? What role does broadcast time play in each case? Which program do you think represents the lowest level of target audience selectivity? Explain your choice.

11-4   TV COMMERCIAL LENGTH: LESS IS MORE?   (343-5)

Commercials have become shorter and shorter as the demand for a limited amount of broadcast time has intensified and advertisers try to get more impressions out of their media budgets. Besides these financial and practical concerns, what other reasons might advertisers have for running shorter TV spots? Base your answer on one of the commercials featured on the MCI Website:

MCI   http://www.mci.com
                Click on Connections, then MCI TV Ad Clips

The MCI TV ad clip collection was chosen for this exercise because it includes thirty-second *and* one-minute versions of the same commercials. Choose one of these ads and watch both versions.

First, describe the central theme and apparent target audience for this commercial. How would you characterize the creative strategy behind this TV spot? Next, write a summary of your gut reactions to both versions of this commercial. Specifically, did the length of each version have a significant impact on your perception and experience of it? If so, how might this variation be exaggerated (or minimized) if you viewed these commercials in a broadcast context?

Finally, discuss the relative strengths and weaknesses of shorter and longer commercials in terms of the following medium-based limitations: fleeting message, clutter, and limited viewer attention. Does the expression "less is more" apply here? Explain.

11-5   TV CLUTTER AND LIMITED VIEWER ATTENTION   (344-5)

This exercise asks you to compare and contrast the broadcast and online versions of ABC News. First, watch this evening's edition of the ABC World News Tonight. Take note of the number and length of commercials shown, the sequence in which they appear, and the way they break up this program's segments. Also consider how different your perception and experience would be if you were watching this program as a normal part of everyday life rather than as an academic exercise. In an ordinary situation, would you pay much attention to the commercials? Next, visit the ABC News Website:

ABC News   http://www.abcnews.com

Peruse this site long enough to get about the same amount of news included in the broadcast edition. Again, pay particular attention to all advertising content, its placement within and around the news, and how these two elements combine to shape your perception and experience.

Finally, compare and contrast these two advertising vehicles in terms of clutter and limited viewer attention. In particular, discuss the different ways in which environmental context and audience motivation can influence advertising effectiveness. Put another way, do people watch the nightly news on TV in the same way and for the same reasons that they might access a news site on the Web? What are the implications of this question for television and Website advertisers? How might new technologies like Internet TV (see Exercise 10-1) change the way we look at this issue?

Using the following cable and network TV Websites for reference, discuss the advantages of advertising on cable television in terms of selectivity. Specifically, what opportunities for **narrowcasting** are offered by the cable stations below? How is this different from the selectivity options offered by the major broadcast networks (see Exercise 11-3)? Cite specific examples to support your answer.

Cable Stations

Lifetime	http://www.lifetimetv.com
The Travel Channel	http://www.travelchannel.com
Univision	http://www.univision.net
The Food Network	http://www.foodtv.com

Broadcast Networks

ABC	http://www.abc.com
CBS	http://www.cbs.com
NBC	http://www.nbc.com
FOX	http://www.foxworld.com

11-7   IMC PERSPECTIVE: DBS SYSTEMS CHALLENGE CABLE   (359)

For the latest news and information on the direct broadcast satellite (DBS) industry, one can turn to the DBS DISH Website:

DBS DISH: Satellite News   http://www.dbsdish.com
& Information

Follow the Latest Sales Figures link and report the current numbers for the three major DBS service providers — DirecTV, Primestar, and EchoStar. Putting these figures together, how many U.S. households now subscribe to one of these DBS services? How does this compare to the figure reported in IMC Perspective 11-2? What rate of growth does this reflect?

Next, follow the Industry News! International link and choose one article that focuses on a current point of competition or conflict between the cable and DBS industries. Summarize the article you found and discuss the possible ramifications of this issue for both sides.

You can always find the latest Nielsen TV ratings by dialing up the following Ultimate TV URL:

Ultimate TV: Nielsen Ratings   http://www.ultimatetv.com/news/nielsen

a)   Follow the Network Primetime link and scroll down to the top twenty ranked programs from last week. Choose one program from this list with which to demonstrate your understanding of the television ratings formulas discussed on p. 361. Use the figures reported for this program along with the estimated total number of **TV households** (reported at the bottom of this homepage) to illustrate the following terms and calculations: **universe estimate**, **program rating**, **ratings point**, **households using television (HUT)**, **share of audience**, and **total audience**. Be sure to include the appropriate mathematical formulas in your answer.

b)   Click on the Cable link to see a list of the top-rated basic and pay cable programs. You will notice that these ratings are significantly lower than those reported for network primetime shows. Discuss the reasons for this significant difference. What are the ramifications of this variation for potential advertisers? ·

c)   Check out the Website for Statistical Research, Inc. (SRI), the firm contracted by the Committee on National Television Audience Measurement to develop an alternative to the Nielsen system.

Statistical Research, Inc.   http://www.sriresearch.com

Follow the S•M•A•R•T link to learn more about the progress of this cooperative venture. Which companies were the latest to offer financial support for this project? What do these organizations stand to gain if the S•M•A•R•T system is adopted as an industry standard? Finally, summarize the most recent developments and advancements in the S•M•A•R•T system that go beyond those described in the main text (see p. 365).

11-9   ADVANTAGES OF RADIO   **(365-8)**

The Radio Advertising Bureau's RadioLink Website contains a wealth of industry information and marketing resources. We suggest you bookmark this site for future use.

Radio Advertising Bureau   http://www.rab.com

To learn more about the advantages of radio advertising, follow the Pro-Radio Publications link. Drawing from these publications, identify and discuss three advantages of radio advertising not covered in the main text. These advantages may reflect entire topic areas not addressed by the authors and/or specific advantages within the following categories: cost and efficiency, selectivity, flexibility, mental imagery, and integrated marketing opportunities. While you may use any of the pro-radio publications featured on this site, we suggest you start with RAB's Radio Marketing Guide & Factbook.

Another useful resource on the RadioLink Website (see Exercise 11-9) is its multi-media coverage of the Radio-Mercury Awards.

Radio Advertising Bureau   http://www.rab.com
                                  Click on <u>Mercury Awards</u>

The Radio-Mercury competition (sponsored by the Radio Creative Fund) is advertising's richest awards show, with more than $225,000 in prize money being given to the creators of the most memorable radio commercials of the past year. Thanks to RealAudio technology, RadioLink allows you to listen to last year's winning entries over the Internet.

Choose one winning commercial from each of the following categories: <u>Humor</u>, <u>Non-humor</u>, <u>Music & Sound Design</u>, <u>Station Produced</u>, and <u>PSA</u>. What is the central theme and apparent target audience for each commercial you chose? Discuss the mental imagery each one strives to create in the minds of radio listeners. Describe the music, sound effects, and/or spoken word elements used to reinforce this imagery in each case.

Finally, do any of these commercials reflect the technique of **image transfer**? If so, define this term and explain why it applies in each case.

Chapter 12:   EVALUATION OF PRINT MEDIA

12-1   *SPIN* GOES ONLINE, BUT WITH A DIFFERENT SPIN (377)

Unless you subscribe to America Online (AOL), you won't be able to access *SPINonline*, the interactive version of the music magazine *Spin*. Though you will find dozens of other music magazines on the Internet, the powers-that-be at *Spin* chose not to create an unrestricted, public Website for their publication. Instead, like dozens of other organizations and publications, they elected to take advantage of the audience-drawing power of AOL, one of the premier commercial online services in North America. *SPINonline* is carried exclusively on AOL, and thus access is limited only to AOL subscribers. To see what sets these online services apart from the broader world of the Internet, take a few moments to peruse the following Websites:

America Online	http://www.aol.com
CompuServe	http://world.compuserve.com
Prodigy	http://www.prodigy.com

First, how do these online services differ from Internet-only service providers? How do their resources compare to the Internet in general and the Web in particular? Given these differences, what are the advantages and disadvantages of running an online publication through one of these services versus maintaining a universal-access Website on the Internet?

Why do you think the publishers of *Spin* chose America Online? Is this choice consistent with what you read about *Spin* in the chapter-opening vignette? How so? What are the potential benefits and pitfalls of this strategy? Do you think it was the right one?

12-2   ADVANTAGES OF MAGAZINES: SELECTIVITY   (382-3)

Discuss the marketing advantages offered by the following magazines in terms of **selectivity**. Be sure to indicate which type(s) of selectivity each publication represents: interest group selectivity, demographic selectivity, and/or geographic selectivity. Do any of these magazines reflect more than one type of selectivity? If so, explain. Cite specific examples (i.e., advertisements) to support your answers.

Buzz Magazine	http://www.buzzmag.com
Nature	http://www.nature.com
New York Magazine	http://www.newyorkmag.com

12-3   ADVANTAGES OF MAGAZINES: CREATIVE FLEXIBILITY   (384-5)

Time Magazine is one of a growing number of major consumer publications being offered in both print and Internet editions. For this exercise, you will need to obtain a recent issue of the print version of *Time* (your school library should have it). Using your copy of *Time* and the following Website for reference, answer the questions below.

Time Magazine	http://www.time.com

Compare and contrast these closely related — but *very* different — advertising vehicles in terms of their creative flexibility. Summarize the options offered by these contrasting versions of *Time* in terms of the type, size, and placement of advertisements they will run. Does the Web version offer online equivalents of any of these print features: **gatefolds**, **bleed pages**, inserts, printaculars, or creative space buys? If so, describe them and explain how they serve the same purposes.

In terms of visual appeal and attention-grabbing potential, which medium is more flexible? Explain your answer.

12-4   ADVANTAGES OF MAGAZINES: CONSUMER RECEPTIVITY   (386)
            AND INVOLVEMENT

Use the following Websites to discuss the advantages of magazine advertising in terms of consumer receptivity and involvement. Which of these two magazines do you think represents a greater advantage in this area? How do the concepts of interest group selectivity and relevance figure into your choice? What are the implications of your analysis for the publishers of general interest magazines and their advertisers?

Saturday Evening Post	http://www.satevepost.org
ELLE	http://www.ellemag.com

As you read in the main text, some magazines are purchased as much for their advertising as for their editorial content. Does either one of these publications fit this description? If so, explain why.

12-5   DISADVANTAGES OF MAGAZINES: CLUTTER AND COMPETITION   (388-90)

Like *Time Magazine* (see Exercise 12-3), *The Atlantic Monthly* is offered in both print and Internet editions. This exercise asks you to examine both versions and discuss the relative disadvantages of these advertising vehicles in terms of clutter and competition. The first step is to obtain a recent issue of the print version of this publication (your school library should have one). With your print copy of *The Atlantic Monthly* in hand, check out the Web version:

> *The Atlantic Monthly*   http://www.theatlantic.com

As you read in the main text, the average consumer magazine contains 48 percent advertising and 52 percent editorial content. How do these alternate versions of *The Atlantic Monthly* compare along these lines? Are print magazine pages comparable to Web pages in terms of advertising space and placement? How so? What role does audience self-guidance and self-pacing play in the processing and filtering of clutter?

Finally, which version of this publication presents more of a clutter problem for advertisers? Cite specific examples to support your answer.

12-6   ETHICAL PERSPECTIVE: IS IT A MAGAZINE OR AN AD?   (389)

Ethical Perspective 12-1 describes how a growing number of companies are getting around the problem of advertising clutter by publishing their own custom magazines. Benetton is one such company, but as you'll see when you visit the Benetton Website, this apparel maker and retailer doesn't want you to associate its publication with its products. Then again…

> Benetton   http://www.benetton.com

Upon entering this site, click the COLORS link to learn about Benetton's custom magazine. What is your gut reaction to Benetton's claim that *Colors* is not an advertising vehicle? Given what you read in Ethical Perspective 12-1, what is your critical analysis of Benetton's approach? As you prepare your response, it may be helpful to read more about this company's unique marketing strategy by following the ADVERTISING link. Also, see Exercise 7-7 for more on Benetton.

(Note to instructors: You can make this exercise even more interesting by obtaining multiple copies of *Colors* to share with your students.)

12-7   PURCHASING MAGAZINE AD SPACE: COST ELEMENTS   (392)

Thanks to its dedicated marketing site, *PC World* provides us with a unique opportunity to consider magazine and online advertising rates side-by-side.

> *PC World*'s Marketing Site   http://marketing.pcworld.com

(exercise continued on following page…)

Follow the appropriate links to view the advertising cost structures for both versions of *PC World*. Summarize and compare the size, color, design, and price options listed on their respective rate cards. Which version of *PC World* offers greater flexibility in terms of cost and exposure frequency? In your discussion, be sure to address the **total audience/readership** estimates for both editions and the role these figures play in setting ad rates.

In terms of cost effectiveness, how might a potential advertiser go about choosing one medium over the other? Based on this, would you expect to find significant differences between the kinds of companies advertising on each version of *PC World*? Explain your answer.

12-8   ADVANTAGES OF NEWSPAPERS: GEOGRAPHIC SELECTIVITY   (400-1)

Discuss the advertising advantages offered by the following newspapers in terms of geographic selectivity. Cite specific examples (i.e., advertisements) from each Website to support your answers. As you list these examples, be sure to indicate why you think each advertiser chose the specific newspaper in question.

Detroit Free Press	http://www.freep.com
South Florida Sun-Sentinel	http://www.sunsentinel.com
San Jose Mercury News	http://www.sjmercury.com
Washington Post	http://www.washingtonpost.com

12-9   LIMITATIONS OF NEWSPAPERS   (402-3)

The *New York Times* was one of the first major newspapers to establish an Internet edition, thereby providing not only expanded coverage and other resources for its readers, but also an exciting new marketing medium for its advertisers. This exercise asks you to consider the differences between the print and online versions of the *New York Times* in terms of the limitations discussed on pp. 402-3. First, obtain a recent issue of the print version. Next, take a few moments to familiarize yourself with its corresponding Website:

New York Times	http://www.nytimes.com

First, compare and contrast these advertising vehicles in terms of the following limitations: poor reproduction, short life span, lack of selectivity, and clutter. As always, cite specific examples to support your analysis.

Next, access the *Online Media Kit* by clicking the AD INFO sidebar attached to the banner at the bottom of the main page. Read about the targeting and reporting capabilities offered through this site by following the appropriate links. Which of these capabilities are unique to the Web environment (i.e., not available through the print edition)? Which are common to both media? Finally, can you think of any capabilities along these lines that are unique to the print edition?

**12-10   IMC PERSPECTIVE: NEWSPAPERS TURN TO RELATIONSHIP   (408)
          MARKETING IN TOUGH TIMES**

Like its counterpart at *PC World* (see Exercise 12-7), the *Wall Street Journal*'s advertising sales department maintains a Website devoted entirely to marketing opportunities and services:

> *Wall Street Journal*:   http://adsales.wsj.com
> Advertising Sales

How does this site reflect the kinds of relationship marketing strategies discussed in IMC Perspective 12-3? Cite at least two specific examples to support your answer. How is this approach different from traditional newspaper ad sales?

Chapter 13: SUPPORT MEDIA

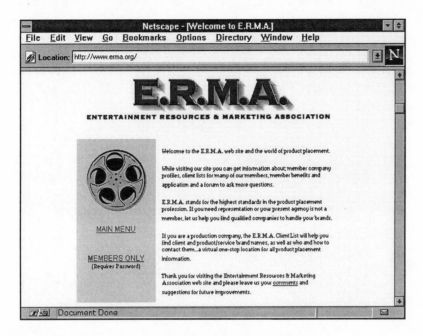

13-1   ADS BECOME THE NEW STARS IN MOVIES AND TV   (413)

Picking up where the chapter-opening vignette left off, let's visit the Entertainment Resources and Marketing Association (ERMA) homepage to learn more about product placement:

>   Entertainment Resources and   http://www.erma.org
>   Marketing Association (ERMA)

First, what is the purpose of ERMA? Describe ERMA's relationship with its "clients" and "members"? Give a specific example of each to illustrate your answer.

Next, follow the link labeled Product Placement Benefits and read the attached article in its entirety. (*Note: to view successive pages of this article, click the right-arrow button at the bottom of the screen.*) Finally, answer the following questions:

>   Does this article discuss any strategic advantages of **product placement** that were not covered in the chapter-opening vignette? If so, what are they?

>   This piece also addresses a handful of potential problems advertisers need to be aware of in terms of selecting agencies and specific product placement strategies. Identify and summarize these cautionary points, or *no-no's*.

>   List all the real-world examples of product placement mentioned in this article.

Exercise 9-9 asked you to examine the television advertising created for Apple Computer's "Think different" campaign. This time you will explore the different types of **out-of-home advertising** that Apple has integrated into its media mix.

Apple   http://www.apple.com

First, click on the "Think different" link. After reading Steve Jobs' letter to Apple employees outlining the philosophy behind this campaign, follow the "Think different" Ad Campaign Photography link to reveal a collection of Apple's latest out-of-home advertisements.

Prepare an annotated list of these ads indicating the specific type of out-of-home media used in each case. In what ways do these ads reflect the creative strategy and brand imaging central to this campaign? Discuss the strategic and creative differences between these ads and the television commercial you analyzed in Exercise 9-9.

Finally, go back to the page featuring Steve Jobs' letter to the Apple community. At the bottom of this page you will find a list of cities in which Apple's out-of-home ads have been (or will be) displayed. How do the cities selected for this aspect of the campaign reflect Apple's target audience? Discuss the pros and cons of using out-of-home advertising to reach this target market.

13-3   OUTDOOR ADVERTISING   **(414-7)**

Let's go back to the Advertising World Website we first visited in Exercise 1-4.

Advertising World   http://advweb.cocomm.utexas.edu/world

From the main index, choose Outdoor & Signs and then click on the *Out-of-Home Advertising Archive* link. This is a collection of outdoor advertising from 1992 to the present compiled by Gannett Outdoor Advertising and the University of Texas at Austin Advertising Department. The Archive is searchable by advertiser, category, geographical location, and keyword. The purpose of the site is to provide an educational and informative resource for students, faculty, and other people interested in outdoor advertising.

Go to the Product Index and choose three products representing a diversity of industries. Just as you did in Exercise 13-2, identify the specific type of out-of-home advertising used to promote each product. Discuss the primary advantages and disadvantages of outdoor advertising that apply most directly in each case. How does the type of product being advertised figure into your analysis? What does this say about the flexibility of the outdoor medium for advertising a wide range of products and services?

13-4   MOBILE BILLBOARDS   **(418)**

Identify and describe the **mobile billboard** highlighted on the Oscar Mayer Website:

Oscar Mayer   http://www.oscar-mayer.com

List three specific media events at which this mobile billboard has been featured. What unique advantages of this medium do these scenarios demonstrate?

How is this advertising vehicle being used in conjunction with other Oscar Mayer promotional programs? In what way does this reflect an integrated marketing communications (IMC) approach?

13-5   IN-STORE MEDIA   **(418-9)**

Let's take a closer look at one of the **in-store media** firms listed in Figure 13-4, ActMedia:

ActMedia   http://www.actmedia.com

Click on the flashing Product Guide and choose one of the ActMedia programs highlighted in Figure 13-4. Summarize the features and selling points enumerated under the headings *Program Details*, *Key Benefits*, *Coverage*, and *Results/Performance*.

How does point-of-purchase advertising influence potential buyers in ways that traditional media-based advertising (i.e., TV/radio commercials, newspaper space ads, and billboards) cannot? Why are these advertising vehicles especially effective in supermarkets? (Can you imagine the same in-store program being used at an auto dealership or furniture store?)

Have you ever encountered this type of ad at your local supermarket or retail store? If so, describe your reaction(s) to it. Can you identify any disadvantages of this in-store media option?

13-6   TRANSIT ADVERTISING   **(421-4)**

The cutting-edge Website created by The Gap gives us a unique opportunity to experience **transit advertising** through the three-dimensional magic of QuickTime VR.

The Gap   http://www.gap.com

First, click on the outdoor advertising link, which can be found both on the main page and the advertising page. Choose the New York City option and then click on the Grand Central QuickTime VR Gallery. To experience these "virtual reality" videos, you will need the QuickTime VR plug-in. If this plug-in is not already installed on your system, you can download it by clicking on the appropriate link at the bottom of this page.

(exercise continued on following page...)

After viewing one of these videos, how would you classify this media vehicle in terms of the three types of transit advertising discussed on pp. 422-3? Use this ad to illustrate the benefits and limitations of transit advertising. Can you think of any advantages that this specific type of transit advertising has over the other two? If so, explain.

13-7   PROMOTIONAL PRODUCTS MARKETING   (424-7)

The Promotional Products Association International (PPA) has created a remarkable Website called the Promotion Clinic. This site features a wealth of **promotional products marketing** resources, including a showcase entitled Weekly Prescriptions, which highlights a wide variety of real-world applications of this support medium.

PPA's Promotion Clinic   http://www.promotion-clinic.ppa.org

Once you have accessed the above URL, click on the <u>DOCTOR</u> link. As you will see, the companies featured in the Weekly Prescriptions showcase are divided into five categories. Identify and describe these five categories. What does this demonstrate about the flexibility of promotional products marketing?

Choose one of these promotional programs and write a brief summary of its main components. Cite specific examples from this case study to illustrate the advantages and disadvantages of promotional products marketing (see pp. 426-7).

13-8   YELLOW PAGES ADVERTISING   (427-9)

Like the magazines and newspapers featured in the exercises for Chapter 12, an online version of the **Yellow Pages** is now available. Check out BigYellow at the following URL:

BigYellow   http://www.bigyellow.com

Execute a few basic searches to get a better sense of the function, scope, and advertising content of this extensive interactive directory. You should also peruse the links listed under the "Advertise" heading to get a better sense of all the advertising options available through BigYellow.

What are the key differences between this Website and the traditional Yellow Pages? Considering these factors, do you think that BigYellow, like its print predecessor, is best described as a **directional medium**? Why or why not? If possible, cite specific examples to support your answer.

Exercise 13-1 introduced you to ERMA, a not-for-profit industry organization dedicated to **product placement**. Now let's turn our attention to a for-profit agency that specializes in this type of marketing — Creative Entertainment Services (CES):

> Creative Entertainment Services   http://www.acreativegroup.com/ces.html

First, make a list of all product placements featured on the CES homepage. In each case, describe the relationship between the product and the film or TV show in which it appears. Specifically, do you think there is a particular reason why these products were placed in these films/shows? Or do these relationships seem arbitrary and based purely on maximum product exposure? Given your answers to the preceding questions, what do you think are the major challenges faced by advertisers and their agencies in terms of choosing an appropriate film or TV show for placement of a particular product?

Next, click on <u>INFO</u> and follow the appropriate link to learn more about the specific <u>SERVICES</u> offered by CES. In terms of industry analysis, background research, and script evaluation, what does this agency do to ensure the effectiveness of its product placements? What kinds of ancillary marketing services are also available in conjunction with these core functions?

13-10   PLACE-BASED MEDIA   (436)

One of the **place-based media** ventures outlined in Figure 13-12 is the Channel One Network, now owned and operated by K-III Communications. To learn more about the purpose, scope, and features of this media service, access the following URL:

> K-III Communications: http://www.k-iii.com/education/channel1/CHANNEL1.HTML
> Channel One overview

Identify and describe the audience for Channel One programming. Based on this description, what types of products and services would you expect to see advertised on this network?

Next, take a few moments to explore the Channel One Website:

> Channel One   http://channelone.com

Prepare a descriptive list of all the advertisers you can find on this Website. Do these companies market the kinds of products and services you expected to see here? Explain your answer.

Finally, discuss the ethical issues surrounding this particular implementation of place-based media advertising. With these issues in mind, imagine that you are in charge of the advertising program for a company whose target market matches Channel One's captive audience. Would you consider using this medium to reach them? Why or why not?

Chapter 14: DIRECT MARKETING AND MARKETING ON THE INTERNET

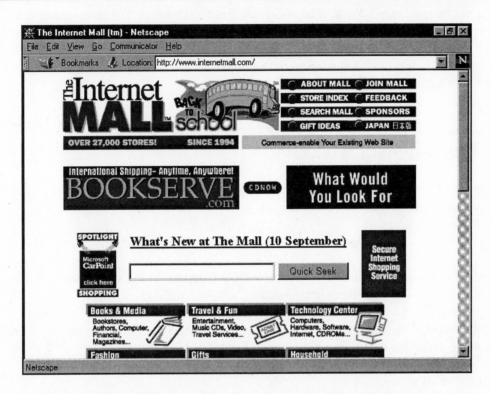

14-1   INTERNET SHOPPING: WILL IT EVER LIVE UP TO THE HYPE?   (439)

Let's consider the question posed at the end of this chapter's opening vignette: "Will the Internet be the catalog of the 1990's, or will it change the way consumers shop forever?" Initial industry feedback indicates that consumers simply are not flocking to the Internet to spend their money. While millions of people do, indeed, "surf the Web" and exchange countless e-mail messages every day, actual on-line purchases have lagged well behind predicted rates. But why?

First, what is your personal take on this mode of commerce? Have you ever made an online purchase? Have you ever been tempted, but held back for some reason? Or are you 100% opposed to the idea? Whatever the case, summarize your personal opinion on this topic. If you resist online purchases for any reason, what (if anything) about this mode of exchange would have to change in order for you to reconsider your stance? What do you think holds most people back from purchasing products and services online?

Next, compare and contrast shopping on the Internet with shopping at a shopping mall. Base your discussion on both your own past shopping mall experiences and your reactions to the following Websites:

(exercise continued on following page...)

The Internet Mall	http://www.internetmall.com
iMall	http://www.imall.com
CyberShop	http://209.67.3.40/store/store.hmx

Of all the differences you noticed, which ones do you think best account for consumers' resistance to making online purchases? What, if anything, are these Web-based companies doing to overcome these barriers?

If you were initially resistant to making an online purchase, has this exercise made you more open to this mode of exchange? Why or why not?

14-2   DEFINING DIRECT MARKETING   (440-1)

Go to the Open Text Index and execute a few keyword searches related to an area of personal interest (professional, recreational, academic, etc.).

The Open Text Index   http://index.opentext.net

Pay particular attention to the banner advertisements that appear during your search. When one of these banners peaks your curiosity, click on it.

Do either (or both) of these marketing vehicles — the banner ad and its corresponding Website — conform to the definition of **direct marketing** on p. 440?

If not ➜ Why not?

If so ➜ Use the relevant banner and/or Website to illustrate the aforementioned definition. What does this demonstrate about key differences between direct marketing and other types of advertising?

14-3   THE ROLE OF DIRECT MARKETING IN THE IMC PROGRAM   (442-4)

The authors have outlined four common ways in which direct marketing activities support and are supported by other elements of the promotional mix (see pp. 442-4). How has the following company capitalized on these kinds of opportunities? As always, cite specific examples to support your answer.

Lotus Development Corporation   http://www.lotus.com

(Note: Explore this site *thoroughly* before answering the above question. Like so many other computer-related Websites, the Lotus site is chock full of integrated advertising content.)

14-4   DIRECT-MARKETING MEDIA   (447-53)

Identify and describe all of the **direct marketing media** reflected in the following Websites. To review, the direct marketing media listed in the main text are direct mail, catalogs, broadcast media, infomercials, teleshopping, print media, telemarketing, and electronic teleshopping.

Insurance Shopping Network	http://www.800insureme.com
Tweeds	http://www.tweeds.com
Excalibur Enterprises	http://www.excaliburmail.com
tvshopping.com	http://www.tvshopping.com

Do any of these Websites represent an integration of two or more of these media? If so, explain.

14-5   DIRECT MAIL ON THE INTERNET — SPAM!   (447-9)

Chances are that you've already been *spammed*, but you may not know it. *Spam* is Internet-speak for unsolicited direct mail advertising received via e-mail (or through a Usenet newsgroup). This is the Internet's version of junk mail, and it has been the source of extensive debate.

Just about any Internet advertising publication will warn you about the dangers of direct e-mail marketing. In general, the Internet community is much more hostile toward electronic junk mail than the general public is toward junk mail delivered by the U.S. Postal Service. Unsolicited e-mail has long been considered a breach of *netiquette* (i.e., Internet etiquette) and a quick and easy way to give your company a bad reputation. Despite this widespread opposition, hundreds (if not thousands) of advertisers still use *spam* to sell their products. Meanwhile, companies specializing in direct e-mail marketing services — especially e-mail address database management — continue to flourish.

Using your own experience and the following Websites for reference, answer the questions below:

ANTI direct e-mail marketing groups

spam.abuse.net	http://spam.abuse.net
CAUCE	http://www.cauce.org

PRO direct e-mail marketing groups

Internet Mail Consortium	http://www.imc.org
The Association for Internet Marketing	http://www.taim.org

Summarize the main arguments on both sides of the *spam* debate. What is your personal opinion regarding this issue? Would you ever consider using this marketing tool? Why or why not?

What are the strategic advantages and disadvantages of direct e-mail advertising? How do these differ from the advantages and disadvantages of traditional direct mail advertising (if at all)?

14-6   ADVANTAGES AND DISADVANTAGES OF DIRECT MARKETING   (455-7)

First, as you did in Exercise 14-4, identify and describe the direct marketing medium reflected in the following Website.

CD Universe   http://www.cduniverse.com

Next, use examples from this site to discuss the advantages and disadvantages of direct marketing listed on pp. 455-7. Which of these strategic issues are especially pertinent to this particular direct marketing medium? For those issues that are less relevant, identify one direct marketing medium more directly affected by each issue and explain why this is the case.

14-7   WEB OBJECTIVES   (460-1)

To further their diverse Web marketing objectives, many companies choose to create and maintain multiple Websites. You can see this in action by exploring the two Quaker Oats sites below.

Quaker Oatmeal Cereals Homepage   http://www.quakeroatmeal.com
Quaker Oats Company Homepage   http://www.quakeroats.com

Identify and describe the different Web objectives embodied in these sites. Use the categories listed on pp. 460-1 to guide your response. As always, cite specific examples to support your answer.

14-8   MEASURING THE EFFECTIVENESS OF WEB ADVERTISING   (462-3)

As you read on p. 462, Infoseek is one leading Web publisher that has used CPM's to establish its advertising rates. To get a better sense of the advanced targeting and reporting capabilities offered by this company, access the Infoseek site below and choose the <u>Advertise on Infoseek</u> link at the bottom of the main page.

Infoseek   http://www.infoseek.com

Identify and describe the targeting/reporting technology that is the cornerstone of Infoseek's advertising package. Summarize the strategic advantages of this technology.

How does this targeting method differ from the keyword-based system discussed in Exercise 10-5?

14-9   ADVANTAGES AND DISADVANTAGES OF INTERNET ADVERTISING   (464-5)

Go to the Yahoo! Website and execute a series of keyword searches related to an area of personal interest (professional, recreational, academic, etc.).

Yahoo!   http://www.yahoo.com

Pay particular attention to the banner advertisements that appear during your search. When one of these banners peaks your curiosity, click on it. Identify the banner ad you chose and describe the Website it led you to. Were you at all surprised by what you found?

Use this experience as the basis for a discussion of the advantages and disadvantages of Internet advertising listed on p. 464. Wherever applicable, cite specific examples to illustrate these key Web marketing issues.

**14-10   COMBINING INTERNET ADVERTISING WITH   (466)
            IMC PROGRAM ELEMENTS**

Like the direct-response media discussed in the first part of this chapter, Web advertising can be enhanced through integration with other program elements. Identify and describe the media-mix integration strategies evidenced on the following Websites. Cite examples to illustrate each IMC program element you find.

Allegra   http://www.ahhh-allegra.com
Micron Electronics   http://www.micronpc.com

Chapter 15: SALES PROMOTION

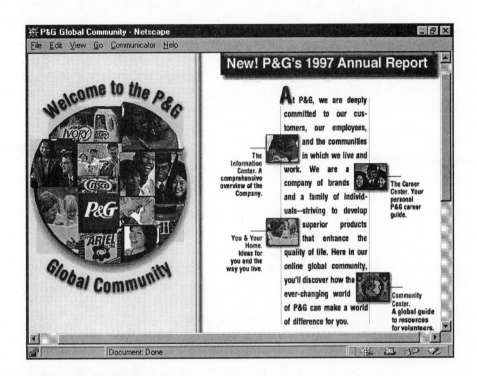

15-1   PROCTER & GAMBLE, SALES PROMOTION, & THE WEB   (469)

As you read in the chapter-opening vignette, Procter & Gamble (P&G) is leading a broad movement to reduce the complexity of **sales promotion** programs. To see what P&G is doing in this area on the Web, let's start by taking a look at their corporate homepage:

Procter & Gamble   http://www.pg.com

Once you have accessed the P&G site, enter the <u>Information Center</u> and choose <u>The Library</u>. From here you can peruse a list of <u>P&G Brands</u> organized by geographical region. As you scan the <u>North American Brands</u> list, notice that many of these brands have their own Websites. Choose three of these brands and answer the questions below. *Note*: Be sure to choose brands with separate and distinct URL's, such as Old Spice (www.oldspice.com) or Sunny Delight (www.sunnyd.com).

For each brand Website, can you find any examples of *sales promotions*?

If so ➔ Identify and describe each sales promotion you found. Do these promotions seem consistent with the P&G simplification strategy outlined in the chapter-opening vignette?

If not ➔ What might account for this omission? Beyond P&G's commitment to simplifying sales promotions (and even eliminating them in some cases), is there anything about the Web medium itself that does not lend itself to this kind of advertising? Further, is there anything about the nature of these specific P&G products that might explain the lack of sales promotions on these sites?

15-2   THE SCOPE AND ROLE OF SALES PROMOTION   (470-1)

Online editions of major newspapers represent a common vehicle for Web-based sales promotions. Explore the *Boston Globe* Website below and click on the first sales promotion banner ad you see.

Boston Globe   http://www.boston.com/globe

First, explain why the ad you chose reflects a **sales promotion**. That is, how does it conform to the definition of this term discussed on p. 470? How do the promotional concepts of *extra incentive* and *acceleration tool* apply in this case?

Finally, is this particular marketing device a **consumer-oriented sales promotion** or a **trade-oriented sales promotion**? Explain your answer.

15-3   CONSUMER FRANCHISE-BUILDING VERSUS   (476-8)
NONFRANCHISE-BUILDING PROMOTIONS

It should come as no surprise that sales promotions are regular features on many electronic teleshopping Websites. To see what one retailer is doing in this area, check out the Staples online catalog:

Staples   http://www.staples.com

First, identify and describe all of the sales promotions you can find on this site. For each example you find, be sure to indicate whether it is a **consumer franchise-building (CFB) promotion** or a **nonfranchise-building (non-FB) promotion**. Use your discussion to illuminate the differences between these two types of sales promotions.

15-4   CONSUMER-ORIENTED SALES PROMOTION: OBJECTIVES   (478-98)
AND TECHNIQUES

Web search engines represent another area of the Internet where sales promotion banner ads are commonplace (see also Exercises 15-2 and 15-3). As one of the most popular search engines, Yahoo! attracts a number of advertisers who regularly use sales promotions to stimulate demand for their products and/or services.

Yahoo!   http://www.yahoo.com

Do some recreational exploring on Yahoo! until a sales promotion banner ad appears (this shouldn't take long at all). Click on the banner to learn more about this promotion and the product/service to which it is connected. Describe both the product/service and the sales promotion. Be sure to indicate and explain the specific promotion technique being used in this case (see pp. 481-98). Which of the following marketing objectives do you think applies here? Explain your choice(s).

- obtaining trial and repurchase
- increasing consumption of an established brand
- defending current customers
- targeting a specific market segment
- enhancing advertising and marketing efforts

Finally, are there any sales promotion techniques that you think are difficult or impossible to execute via the Web? Conversely, are there any techniques that are particularly well-suited to this medium? Explain your answers.

15-5   SAMPLING   (481-4)

How does the following Website capitalize on the sales promotion technique of **sampling**? Cite specific examples to illustrate your answer.

LucasArts   http://www.lucasarts.com

Does this type of sampling correspond to any of the sampling categories listed in the main text? If so, indicate which one and explain why it fits in this category. If not, describe this new technique and discuss its potential for promoting other types of products.

15-6   COUPONING   (484-90)

To see how the sales promotion technique of **couponing** has been applied to the online environment, take a few moments to explore the following Websites:

America's Coupons	http://www.americascoupons.com
Club Coupons	http://www.clubcoupons.com
Super Saver Grocery Coupons	http://www.supersaver-coupons.com
Quick Coupons	http://www.qponz.com

What are the most significant differences between Internet coupons and traditional coupons? Does Web-based distribution of these promotional items alleviate any of the problems with coupons outlined in the main text (see pp. 486-7)? If so, explain how. Conversely, what are the disadvantages of coupon Websites compared to traditional coupon distribution channels (i.e., newspaper inserts, direct mail, magazines, and packages)?

15-7   PREMIUMS   (490-2)

Go to the Quaker State Website below and follow the <u>Consumer Offers and Promotions</u> link.

Quaker State   http://www.quakerstate.com

Which of the sales promotions featured on this page represent **premiums**? Identify and describe all of the premium offers you find. Be sure to indicate whether each one is a **free premium** or a **self-liquidating premium**.

Discuss Quaker State's strategy of combining premiums with celebrity endorsements. In particular, how do target audience factors figure into this approach?

15-8   CONTESTS AND SWEEPSTAKES   (492-5)

The ContestGuide.com Website gives us a unique opportunity to examine dozens of currently running contests and sweepstakes side-by-side.

ContestGuide.com   http://www.contestguide.com

First, find one example of each of the following sales promotions: **contest**, **sweepstakes**, and **game**. Write a brief description of the promotions you chose and explain how they conform to the definitions of these terms in the main text (see pp. 492-4).

Next, make a list of all product and service types represented on this site. This will require you to look at each contest/sweepstakes summary and identify the sponsoring company's product or service category (i.e., broadcast media, software, travel, apparel, etc.). Analyze your results. What were the most common product/service types you found? How might you explain this?

15-9   EVENT SPONSORSHIP   (497-8)

As you read on p. 497, sports receive two-thirds of all monies spent on **event sponsorship**. To see some real-world applications of this sales promotion technique, go to the Ladies Professional Golf Association (LPGA) Website.

Ladies Professional Golf Association   http://www.lpga.com

Once you have accessed the LPGA main page, follow the <u>LPGA tour</u> link and then click on <u>individual tournaments</u>. Identify all of the event sponsorships listed on this page. Why do you think each company chose to sponsor a women's professional golf tournament? How do target audience factors figure into this strategy? Would these advertisers achieve the same marketing goal(s) by sponsoring a men's golf tournament? Or a college football bowl game? Or an auto race? Explain.

Next, go back to the <u>LPGA tour</u> page and click on the <u>promotional partners and licensees</u> link. Read a half dozen or so of the descriptions under this heading. What are the key differences between these types of promotional efforts and the events sponsorships addressed above? Discuss the relative advantages and disadvantages of these contrasting approaches to sports event-related sales promotion.

15-10   TRADE-ORIENTED SALES PROMOTION   (498-506)

Intel, the computer company best known for its Pentium processors and "Intel inside" ad campaign, maintains a trade-oriented Website called Info for the Channel. This specialized site provides Intel resellers (and potential resellers) with a wealth of information, technical support material, dealer incentives, and other resources.

Intel Info for the Channel   http://channel.intel.com
(reseller information)

Follow the <u>programs and promotions</u> link and click on <u>promotions</u>. As you will see, some of this promotional information is password protected and thus only available to registered resellers. Choose one of the unprotected promotion links and answer the following questions.

Identify and describe the **trade-oriented sales promotion** you selected. What specific type(s) of sales promotion does this represent (see pp. 499-505)? Which of the four marketing objectives discussed on pp. 498-9 is exemplified here? Explain your choice(s).

Chapter 16: PUBLIC RELATIONS, PUBLICITY, AND CORPORATE ADVERTISING

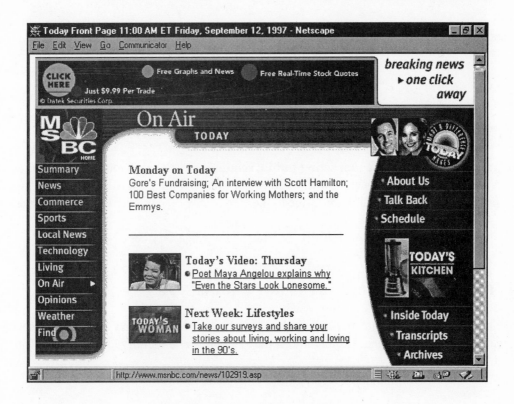

16-1   PUBLICITY STUNTS OR SMART MARKETING?   (513)

As you read in the chapter-opening vignette, dozens of advertisers have capitalized on the **publicity** potential of the *Today* show's open set. But while we know that these advertisers are just trying to get free airtime for their products, why do you think they chose this particular program? To better answer this question, watch one installment of the *Today* show (if possible). For more information on this program, visit the following URL:

Today   http://www.msnbc.com/news/TODAY_front.asp

First, make a list of all the companies mentioned in the vignette as having "crashed" the *Today* show. Why do you think each advertiser chose this program (aside from the obvious answer that they *could*)? What role did target audience factors play in this decision? In your opinion, which of these companies probably benefited most from this tactic? Did any of these companies or products seem mismatched with the *Today* show? Explain your answers.

Can you think of any potential pitfalls in these kinds of publicity stunts? If so, explain.

16-2   THE NEW ROLE OF PR   (514-5)

Figure 16-1 demonstrates four relationships that marketing and **public relations** can assume in an organization. Which relationship class do you think best characterizes each of the following organizations? Justify your choice in each case.

Women's NBA	http://www.wnba.com
United Way	http://www.unitedway.org
Kaiser Permanente	http://www.kaiperm.org
National Enquirer	http://www.nationalenquirer.com

16-3   MARKETING PUBLIC RELATIONS (MPR) FUNCTIONS   (516)

Identify and describe all of the **marketing public relations (MPR)** activities featured on the Ben & Jerry's Website. Be sure to specify the marketing objective behind each MPR function. In other words, how does each MPR effort add value to the Ben & Jerry's integrated marketing program?

Ben & Jerry's   http://www.benjerry.com

16-4   DETERMINING RELEVANT TARGET AUDIENCES   (518-22)

Apple Computer is one of many major corporations using the Web to carry out various aspects of its public relations program. First, explore the Apple site below and identify all of the PR efforts you can find.

Apple Computer   http://www.apple.com

For each PR effort you identify, indicate whether it is directed toward an **internal** or **external audience**. Specifically, which of the following nine target audiences does each effort address?

- employees of the firm
- stockholders & investors
- civic & business organizations
- suppliers & customers
- financial groups
- community members
- the media
- governments
- educators

Were any of these PR elements relevant to more than one group? If so, what does this say about the flexibility of PR as a strategic marketing tool?

16-5   IMPLEMENTING THE PR PROGRAM   (522-4)

Identify and describe all of the public relations tools integrated into the Website created for The Body Shop. Specifically, how many of the tools discussed on pp. 523-4 can you find? To review, these are **press releases**, **press conferences**, **exclusives**, interviews, and community involvement.

The Body Shop   http://www.the-body-shop.com

Did you find any PR elements that do not fit into one of these categories? If so, describe each one, including its apparent objective and target audience.

Considering your responses above, which PR tools are most easily applied to the Web environment? Conversely, are there any tools that seem difficult or impossible to execute using this medium? How might future technological advances open up the Internet as a public relations vehicle?

16-6   ADVANTAGES AND DISADVANTAGES OF PR   (524-6)

The PR Newswire Website represents one way in which the Internet is changing the way public relations are carried out. Explore the various functions of this service and answer the questions below.

PR Newswire   http://www.prnewswire.com

First, outline the overall purpose and features of this site. Identify and describe the various groups that make up its target audience.

How might this vehicle mitigate some of the disadvantages of PR discussed on pp. 524-526? Cite specific examples to support your answer.

16-7   PUBLICITY   (528-31)

To see how one computer manufacturer has capitalized on positive publicity in its online marketing, explore the Dell Website:

Dell Computer   http://www.us.dell.com

Identify and describe one example of **publicity** that Dell has integrated into this advertising-oriented site. Use this example to illuminate the differences between publicity and public relations. Why is this such an effective marketing device for companies like Dell?

16-8   THE CONTROL AND DISSEMINATION OF PUBLICITY   (531)

Because of their impact on the environment, oil companies, mining operations, chemical processors, and lumber mills are often the subjects of negative publicity. Using the conservation Websites below for reference, find a current media item reflecting this kind of negative publicity. Be sure the story you choose involves a major corporation (such as Chevron, Georgia Pacific, Dow Chemical, etc.) that maintains a Website. The news and press release areas of the following sites will be especially helpful in your search.

(exercise continued on following page...)

Environmental Defense Fund	http://www.edf.org
Natural Resources Defense Council	http://www.nrdc.org
Sierra Club	http://www.sierraclub.org
Greenpeace	http://www.greenpeace.org

First, summarize the media item you found. Why does this story represent negative publicity for the company in question and what is its potential impact?

Next, locate and access the Website for the company in question. Does this site contain any direct references to this case of negative publicity?

> If so ➔ Summarize the company response and evaluate its potential effectiveness in minimizing the impact of this "bad press."

> If not ➔ Are there areas of this site that refer to this company's general policies and initiatives in this area? If so, summarize the various elements of this proactive approach to negative publicity control. Cite specific examples to support your answer.

16-9   CORPORATE ADVERTISING: OBJECTIVES AND CRITICISM   (532-4)

Exercises 4-9 and 8-1 focused on the Levi's product-oriented Website, Levi.com. This time you will examine the corporate site for Levi Strauss & Co.

Levi Strauss & Co.   http://www.levistrauss.com

What are the apparent objectives of this **corporate advertising** tool? How would you describe the target audience for this site?

Based on what you see here, how might the marketing managers at Levi Strauss respond to the criticisms of corporate advertising listed on p. 534?

16-10   TYPES OF CORPORATE ADVERTISING   (534-8)

Which type(s) of corporate advertising are reflected in the following Website? To review, the major types are **image advertising**, **advocacy advertising**, and **cause-related marketing**. Cite specific examples to support your answer. *Note*: Be sure not to miss the See Our Ads link.

Archer Daniels Midland Co.   http://www.admworld.com

For any cases of image advertising you identified, which of the methods described on pp. 535-6 were used?

Does this site reflect an integration of two or more of the above techniques? If so, summarize this strategy and discuss why the Web medium is especially well suited to this approach.

Chapter 17: PERSONAL SELLING

17-1   THE BEST SALES FORCES REFLECT AN IMC APPROACH   (543)

To learn more about the top 25 sales forces in the United States as ranked by *Sales & Marketing Management* magazine, go to the following URL:

> *Sales & Marketing Management*   http://www.salesandmarketing.com

Once you have accessed this site's main page, click on the S&MM Magazine button. Look under the heading "*S&MM* exclusive" and choose the America's Best Sales Forces link. Read the article and its accompanying sidebars. When you are done, choose one top-ranked company and answer the questions below. *Note*: For the purposes of this exercise, do *not* choose Dell Computer. We will examine this remarkable company in Exercise 17-2.

First, locate the official Website for the company you chose. Does this site reflect an IMC orientation? If so, cite specific examples to illustrate this approach. Can you find any evidence of relationship marketing on this site? If so, describe these elements and explain their strategic importance in selling this company's products/services.

Finally, have any personal selling functions been integrated into this Website? If so, describe these features. If not, do you think it's even *possible* to execute any kind of personal selling practices via the Web? Explain your answer.

17-2   THE SCOPE AND ROLE OF PERSONAL SELLING   (544-5)

According to *Sales & Marketing Management* magazine, Dell Computer represented the number one sales force in the United States for 1997. Let's use the Dell Website to consider the scope and role of **personal selling**.

> Dell Computer   http://www.us.dell.com

Explore the Dell site thoroughly and see if you can find any instances of personal selling. Be sure to take a close look at their "Build You Own System" option, which allows you to put together a customized order to suit your exact needs and purchase it online. Does this (or any other marketing tool on this site) reflect a personal selling approach? Use your answer to demonstrate your understanding of this term as defined on p. 544. How does this form of communication differ from those presented in Chapters 1-16?

Finally, evaluate the Web as a personal selling medium. How might future technological advancements open up the Web as a vehicle for this marketing tool?

17-3   DETERMINING THE ROLE OF PERSONAL SELLING   (545-6)

As you read on p. 545, the first questions a manager must ask when preparing the promotional program are what the specific responsibilities of personal selling will be and what role it will assume relative to other promotional mix elements. Using Figure17-2 and the four guiding questions discussed on pp. 545-6, evaluate the potential effectiveness of personal selling as a marketing tool for each of the following products/services. That is, how big a role do you think personal selling plays (or should play) for these organizations? Justify your answer in each case while citing specific examples whenever possible.

> Vulcan Industries   http://www.vulcanindustries.com
> Kellogg's Corn Pops   http://www.cornpops.com
> INFeD   http://www.infed.com
> Airborne Express   http://www.airborne-express.com

17-4   RELATIONSHIP MARKETING AND THE NATURE OF   (546-7)
         PERSONAL SELLING

Can you find any examples of **relationship marketing** on the following Website? If so, describe these elements and discuss their strategic importance.

> The Gutter Man, Inc.   http://www.gutterman.com

Which stage of Thomas Wotruba's personal selling evolution (see pp. 546-7) does The Gutter Man represent? Cite examples from the above Website to support your answer. If this company does not reflect Wotruba's *procreator stage*, how might it use **relationship marketing** to transform itself into this type of operation?

17-5   PERSONAL SELLING RESPONSIBILITIES   (548-51)

Visit the following Websites to learn about one of the best-known and longest-running personal selling programs in the United States:

Girl Scouts of the USA	http://www.gsusa.org Click on <u>GS Cookie Sales</u>
ABC Girl Scout Cookie Bakers	http://www.girlscoutcookiesabc.com

Using Figure 17-5 as a guide, how would you classify the personal selling practice that is the cornerstone of this program? Which of these terms — **creative selling**, **order taking**, or **missionary sales** — is most applicable here? Explain your answer.

Describe this organization's salespeople in terms of the six job requirements listed on pp. 548-50. Cite specific examples to support your answer. Discuss the strategic advantage of personal selling for accomplishing this program's mission.

17-6   ADVANTAGES AND DISADVANTAGES OF PERSONAL SELLING   (551-3)

Like Amway, Mary Kay, and Avon, Tupperware's primary marketing vehicle is — and always has been — personal selling. However, all of these companies are discovering the advertising power of the Internet. To see how Tupperware is using the Web to augment its marketing mix, check out the following site.

Tupperware   http://www.tupperware.com

Using this site for reference, discuss the relative advantages and disadvantages of personal selling and Website advertising as marketing tools for Tupperware. Be sure to address the following variables in your analysis:

Advantages of personal selling	*Disadvantages of personal selling*
• allowing for two-way interaction	• inconsistent messages
• tailoring of the message	• sales force/management conflict
• lack of distraction	• high cost
• involvement in the decision process	• poor reach
	• potential ethical problems

You may have noticed that Tupperware does *not* give Web users the option of ordering and/or purchasing its products online. What might explain this? Which of the disadvantages listed above may apply here? Explain.

17-7 COMBINING PERSONAL SELLING WITH OTHER (553-7)
PROMOTIONAL TOOLS

As you read on p. 553, personal selling is rarely, if ever, used alone. Rather, this promotional tool both supports and is supported by other components of the integrated marketing communications program. For a real-world example of this integrated approach, take a look at the Avon Website:

> Avon   http://www.avon.com

Identify and describe all of the promotional mix elements you can find on this Website. Discuss how each promotional tool can be used to support Avon's personal selling program and vice versa.

Unlike the Tupperware Website (see Exercise 17-6), Avon's site allows Web users to order and purchase its products online. Does this in any way undermine Avon's personal selling program? If you were an Avon sales representative, how might you view this situation? Explain your answers.

Chapter 18: MEASURING THE EFFECTIVENESS OF THE PROMOTIONAL PROGRAM

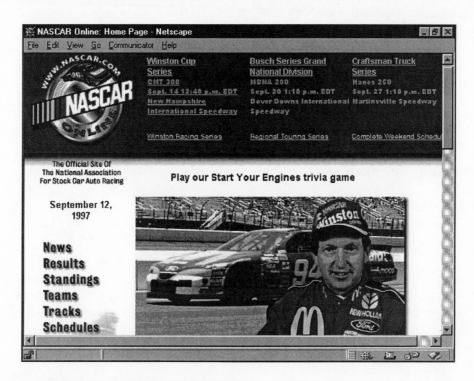

18-1 NASCAR SPONSORSHIPS TAKE OFF (563)

Take one look at the main page of the official NASCAR Website and you'll see dozens of corporate sponsorships in action. Whether they are sponsoring a major competition, a driving team, or a racetrack, advertisers have long appreciated and capitalized on the marketing potential of the NASCAR world. Check out the NASCAR homepage below and answer the following questions:

NASCAR   http://www.nascar.com

a) Make a list of all the corporate sponsorships you can find by following the <u>TEAMS</u> and <u>SCHEDULES</u> links. Be sure to include all driver and race sponsors in both sections. Next, divide this list by sponsor product type. This will require you to create separate lists under headings like automotive, food/beverage, and any other applicable categories. When you are done, discuss your results. Which product type was most common? What might explain this? Were there any sponsorships that surprised you? Explain. Was there any overall difference between race sponsors and team sponsors? Discuss the relative strengths and weaknesses of these two sponsorship strategies.

b) Citing specific examples from the NASCAR site, demonstrate your knowledge of the following concepts: media equivalencies, exposures, image, and brand awareness.

18-2   MEASURING ADVERTISING EFFECTIVENESS: WHAT TO TEST   (566-8)

Discuss how the four components of the communications model — source, message, media, and receiver — could help Trump Hotels & Casino Resorts determine the primary evaluation criteria for its Website (i.e., *what to test*). Use the four subject headings listed on pp. 567-8 to organize your response. Be sure to address this site's objective, target audience, and creative strategy in your answer. In basic terms, what specific type of advertising does this site represent?

Trump Hotels &   http://www.trump.com
Casino Resorts

With regard to media strategies, how does the **vehicle option source effect** apply in this case?

18-3   THE TESTING PROCESS   (571-85)

Figure 18-11 outlines the major components of ASI Market Research's *recall-plus test*. To learn about the full range of services offered by this firm, visit the ASI Website.

ASI Market Research, Inc.   http://www.asiresearch.com

Click on the ASI Products and Services link and read the brief introduction. Then choose one of the program offerings listed under the heading Advertising Research. (*Note*: For the purposes of this exercise, do *not* choose the *recall-plus test* covered in the main text.) Use the measurement program you selected as the basis for answering the following questions.

a) Identify and describe the measurement/evaluation program you chose. Using Figure 18-11 as a guide, outline the objective, method, and output of this research tool.

b) Which one of the testing categories listed on pp. 571-585 best characterizes this program? Justify your choice.

c) According to ASI, what are the key benefits of this service? Can you see any limitations or potential pitfalls in this program? If so, describe them. Can you suggest any strategies for overcoming these weaknesses?

For more on ASI Market Research, see Exercise 18-4.

18-4   APPLYING THE TESTING PROCESS TO INTERACTIVE MEDIA   (572-85)
   AND THE WEB

Picking up where Exercise 18-3 left off, let's now consider ASI's research offerings that are geared toward interactive media and the Web.

ASI Market Research, Inc.   http://www.asiresearch.com

Again, follow the <u>ASI Products and Services</u> link, but this time click on <u>Interactive/WWW Research</u>. After you have read the brief introduction to ASI Interactive, explore the various components of this service. *Note*: For the purposes of this exercise, you should skip the Custom Research option.

First, prepare an outline summarizing the objectives, methods, and outputs of these research tools. Again, use Figure 18-11 as a framework for constructing your outline.

Next, discuss the similarities and differences between these interactive media measures and the traditional media (print ad, TV commercial) evaluation techniques covered in the main text. Would you say that ASI's program treats promotional Websites more like print ads or TV commercials? Explain your answer and discuss the broader implications of this question for measuring the advertising effectiveness of interactive media.

18-5   PRETESTING OF FINISHED ADS   (574-8)

To get a better sense of the current audio/visual capabilities of the Internet, take some time to explore the following cutting-edge Websites.

Pepsi World   http://www.pepsi.com
The Gap   http://www.gap.com

As you can see, these companies have capitalized on the latest advancements in Web-based animation, video, audio, and interactive graphics. Considering these ever-expanding possibilities, how could advertisers like Pepsi and The Gap use their Websites to **pretest** finished print ads and broadcast commercials? Specifically, how might **portfolio tests**, **dummy advertising vehicles**, and **theater tests** be adapted to the Web environment? Sketch a rough outline of how each of these tests could be executed using the Web. Be sure to discuss not only the relevant technical and interactive design issues, but also the key research methodology factors (i.e., sampling, bias, environmental control, etc.).

What are the potential advantages and disadvantages of using the Web to conduct these kinds of pretests? What roles do sampling factors and situational variables play in your analysis?

Finally, could the Internet mitigate any of the disadvantages of these research methods discussed on pp. 574-6? Explain.

18-6   MARKET TESTING OF ADS   (578-85)

For the purposes of this exercise, select any advertising-oriented Website upon which to base your responses to the following questions. If you have trouble coming up with a site that interests you, we suggest you peruse the company index at the back of this exercise book. You may also wish to consult one of the search engines used earlier in this course.

(*exercise continued on following page…*)

First, identify and describe the company you chose, including its primary products/services. Characterize the target audience, creative strategy, and apparent marketing objectives of this Website.

If you were responsible for market testing the advertising effectiveness of your chosen Website, which of the **posttests** listed on pp. 578-85 would be most useful in your research? That is, which print and broadcast ad posttests are most applicable and adaptable to Website advertising evaluation? Conversely, which are least relevant? As you prepare your response, consider how you might combine these measurement tools to take advantage of the most pertinent aspects of each.

What does your analysis say about the similarities and differences between the Web and each of the two traditional media (print and broadcast) in terms of measuring promotional effectiveness?

18-7   MEASURING THE EFFECTIVENESS OF WEBSITE ADVERTISING: (563-90) A CHAPTER REVIEW

The online version of *Advertising Age* magazine features a collection of Website reviews called CyberCritiques.

> *Advertising Age*   http://adage.com

To access these reviews, follow the <u>INTERACTIVE</u> link and then click on <u>CyberCritiques</u>. Choose one of these reviews and answer the questions below. If possible, select a critique that focuses on a Website with which you are not already familiar.

First, identify and describe the organization in question, including its products/services, target audience, and apparent Web marketing objective(s). Does the critique address this organization's entire site or one particular element in its Web marketing mix?

Do you agree with this reviewer's assessment? Explain your response. Also, discuss the limitations of relying on this kind of subjective, "expert" review to judge the appropriateness and potential effectiveness of online advertising.

Finally, using everything you have learned in Chapter 18, outline a plan for measuring the effectiveness of this Web advertising initiative. Your outline should address the key concepts and practices from this chapter that are most applicable in this case. Be sure to describe any resources outside of the firm that would be helpful in your assessment.

Chapter 19: BUSINESS-TO-BUSINESS COMMUNICATIONS

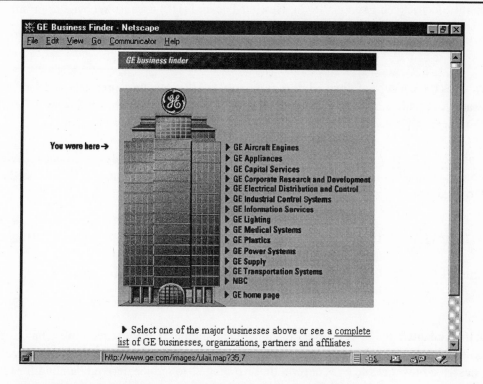

19-1   CONSUMER MARKETERS GO BUSINESS-TO-BUSINESS   (595)

As you can see in the above graphic taken from the General Electric Website, the four GE services mentioned in the chapter-opening vignette (Capital Services, Medical Systems, Aircraft Engines, Power Systems) are but a few of the dozen-plus business service divisions of this high-tech giant. Let's visit this site to see how GE is using the Web to promote these services.

General Electric   http://www.ge.com

First, follow the In Business with GE link and scan the options under this heading. Then click on the appropriate link to Visit a GE business site. Choose one of these divisions and summarize its products and services. Use examples from this division's Web pages to demonstrate your understanding of the term **business-to-business communications** as defined on p. 596.

Finally, go back to the GE main page and click on the At Home with GE link. Explore this area, paying particular attention to the creative strategies used to promote GE's consumer products. Discuss the similarities and differences between this approach and that used to execute the GE business-to-business promotion you examined earlier in this exercise. Do you think that the similarities you noted were at all a result of GE wanting its Website to have a consistent look and feel throughout? Explain you answer. If you agree with this analysis, how might this creative strategy work against the marketing managers who are trying to promote their various products and services in the most appropriate and effective manner possible?

19-2 DIFFERENCES BETWEEN BUSINESS & CONSUMER   **(596-600)**
COMMUNICATIONS

Like General Electric (see Exercise 19-1), Hewlett-Packard (HP) uses its Website to promote
products and services directed toward both consumer and business markets.

Hewlett-Packard   http://www.hp.com

First, how does the concept of **derived demand** apply to HP's business products and services?
Demonstrate your understanding of this term using examples from the above Website. Be sure to
explain why derived demand does *not* propel the market for HP's consumer products.

Next, citing examples from the HP site above, demonstrate as many of the differences between
business and consumer communications as you can. Use the nine key characteristics listed on pp.
596-600 to organize your response.

19-3 GLOBAL PERSPECTIVE: INTEL TAKES ITS CAMPAIGN WORLDWIDE   **(597)**

Picking up where Global Perspective 19-1 left off, let's check out the Intel Website:

Intel   http://www.intel.com

How has Intel adapted its "Intel Inside" consumer campaign to the Web medium? That is, discuss
the ways in which this site reflects the marketing strategies discussed in Global Perspective 19-1.
Further, describe how this site goes *beyond* those strategies to induce derived demand for Intel's
products.

Does Intel also use this site to conduct business-to-business communications? If so, identify and
describe the specific features designed to carry out this function.

Based on what you've learned about this company's advertising, would you say that Intel represents
an integrated marketing communications (IMC) approach? Explain your answer.

19-4 DEVELOPING BUSINESS-TO-BUSINESS PROMOTIONAL   **(601-9)**
STRATEGIES: USING AN OUTSIDE AD AGENCY

The following advertising agency specializes in business-to-business communications.

Bazzirk, Inc.   http://www.bazzirk.com

First, summarize the services offered by Bazzirk, Inc. Organize these services in terms of the major
program elements listed under the heading "Implementing the Business-to-Business Program" (pp.
602-9). Which of these elements does Bazzirk emphasize most in its Website advertising? Does
Bazzirk offer any special services that a consumer advertising-oriented agency would not? If so,
identify them and explain why they are only applicable within the context of business-to-business
advertising.

19-5   IMPLEMENTING THE BUSINESS-TO-BUSINESS PROGRAM: (602-3)
RADIO ADVERTISING

The Lotus Development Corporation Website gives us a unique opportunity to listen to a few business-to-business radio commercials via the Internet.

Lotus Development Corp.   http://www.lotus.com

Once you have accessed the Lotus main page, follow the <u>Media Catalog</u> link and choose the Media Files list organized <u>by Content Category</u>. Then click on <u>Commercials</u> to reveal a collection of Lotus radio spots you can download. After listening to all of the available files, choose one commercial upon which to base your answers to the following questions.

First, identify and describe the Lotus product featured in this radio spot. Is it clear from the commercial what this product actually does, or did you have to look elsewhere on this site to get a better sense of its capabilities? If you had to consult other resources, what limitation of radio advertising does this demonstrate? Do you think this represents a significant problem for Lotus in promoting this product? Explain.

Next, what is the target audience for this ad? Based on your answer to this question, in which geographical areas and at what times of day would you expect this commercial to air? With these issues in mind, discuss the relative advantages and disadvantages of using TV commercials and radio spots to reach this target audience.

Finally, describe both the appeal style and central message of this ad. In terms of its creative strategy, is this commercial significantly different from consumer-oriented radio advertising? Explain your answer.

19-6   IMC PERSPECTIVE: TV GAINS POPULARITY WITH BUSINESS   (605)
MARKETERS

Let's revisit the MCI television commercials we examined earlier in Exercises 8-10 and 11-4.

MCI   http://www.mci.com
          Click on <u>Connections</u>, then <u>MCI TV Ad Clips</u>

Do any of these commercials represent business-to-business advertising? If so, identify and describe each TV spot that fits this description. Of those you singled out, are these ads targeted exclusively at a business audience, or do they also serve a consumer-oriented promotional function? Explain. Cite specific commercial content to support you answer. What are the implications of your analysis with regard to selecting media and creative strategies for business-to-business marketing?

Finally, how do the advantages and disadvantages of TV advertising covered in IMC Perspective 19-2 apply here?

19-7   THE INTERNET AND BUSINESS-TO-BUSINESS COMMUNICATION   (606-7)

As we have seen throughout this chapter's exercises, the Internet has become a popular and powerful tool for business-to-business marketing. Let's consider the unique benefits of this medium by looking at the Xerox Website below.

Xerox   http://www.xerox.com

Identify and describe the various promotional strategies that Xerox has integrated into this remarkable site. Specifically, can you find online applications of direct marketing, sales promotions, incentives, public relations, and/or trade show-related advertising? If so, cite specific examples of these strategies.

Considering everything you have learned in this chapter, which aspects and capabilities of the Web medium make it especially well suited to business-to-business advertising?

**19-8   EVALUATING PROMOTIONAL EFFORTS: USING THE COPY   (612-3)
          CHASERS EVALUATION CRITERIA**

Evaluate IBM's *e-business* Website according to the Copy Chasers criteria listed in Figure 19-14.

IBM: *e-business*   http://www.ibm.com/e-business

In which of these ten evaluative areas does this site excel? For those areas you judged negatively, suggest specific strategies for improvement. Were any of these deficiencies based on the limitations of the Web medium itself? If so, explain.

Chapter 20: INTERNATIONAL ADVERTISING AND PROMOTION

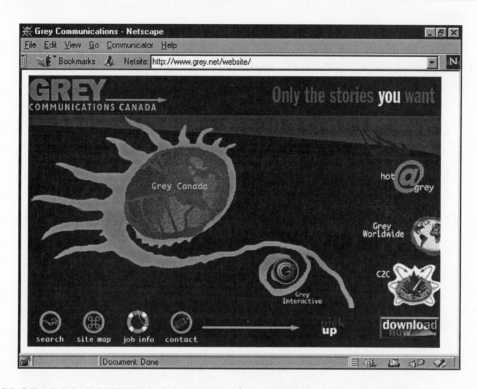

20-1 GLOBAL MARKETERS GO WITH ONE IMAGE, ONE AGENCY (615)

As you read in the chapter-opening vignette, many multinational corporations are consolidating their global marketing by choosing one agency to handle all (or most) of their consumer and business advertising. We can see this trend in action by visiting the Website for Grey Communications of Canada.

Grey Communications of Canada	http://www.grey.net

Once you have accessed this site, follow the Grey Worldwide link and choose Worldwide Clients to see an annotated list of this agency's primary global accounts. Choose two of these companies and locate their independent Websites. As you explore these sites, answer the following questions with regard to *both* clients.

Identify and describe all of the globally oriented marketing elements you can find. Do these elements promote a unified, consistent product image to an international audience? If so, how? If not, how do you account for any message variation you found? Can you find any potential pitfalls in these Web-based global marketing efforts? If so, explain.

(exercise continued on following page...)

What are the major strategic advantages for both companies in selecting one agency for all of their global advertising efforts? Is there anything about their products that makes this choice especially apt?

Finally, why is it particularly important for Website advertisers to be sensitive to international marketing issues?

20-2   GLOBAL PERSPECTIVE: JUST DOING IT GLOBALLY   (622)

Consider this excerpt from Global Perspective 20-1:

> The award-winning "Nike vs. Evil" spot from [Wieden & Kennedy's]
> Amsterdam office, in which Nike's soccer endorsers do battle with
> Satan, reflects Nike's belief that it must dominate soccer to have
> global credibility.

Explore the following site to see how Nike is using the Web to carry out its soccer marketing strategy:

Nike   http://www.nike.com

Identify and describe the major elements of Nike's soccer-related Website advertising. In particular, would you say that this effort has an international emphasis? If so, how? Does Nike run the risk of alienating its American customers by integrating global content into its soccer advertising? Explain your answer.

 Now let's take a look at how two of Nike's foreign-based competitors, Adidas and Mizuno, have adapted their soccer-related promotional programs to the Web.

Adidas   http://www.adidas.com
Mizuno   http://www.mizunousa.com

Compare and contrast these efforts with Nike's. Which company do you think has made the best use of the Web medium as a vehicle for international soccer-related advertising? Explain your answer.

20-3   GLOBAL VERSUS LOCALIZED ADVERTISING   (625-33)

Would you say that the following Website reflects **global marketing** as defined on p. 625? Before you respond, be sure to explore this site *thoroughly*, including its various regional links. Use your answer to demonstrate your understanding of the terms **global marketing** and **global advertising**.

Canon   http://www.canon.com

If you said that this site *does* reflect a global marketing approach, can you find any examples of **pattern advertising**? If so, what are they and what are the advantages of this strategy?

114

20-4   GLOBAL PERSPECTIVE: TEENS — A NEW GLOBAL MARKET SEGMENT   (631)

Global Perspective 20-2 highlights MTV as one advertising vehicle that has helped expand global markets for companies targeting teenage consumers. This New York-based video music network is watched in nearly 100 countries and is tremendously popular in Europe, reaching almost 60 million households.

But beyond MTV's unique standing as a venue for teen-oriented advertisers, how does this network promote *itself* in different regions around the world? Just because MTV speaks one of the "universal languages" of teens — music — does this mean that it can use a single, uniform message to reach all segments of its worldwide audience? To answer this question, take some time to peruse the following MTV Websites:

MTV Online (USA)	http://www.mtv.com
MTV Europe	http://www.mtveurope.com
MTV Asia	http://www.mtvasia.com
MTV Australia	http://www.village.com.au/mtv

As you consider the similarities and differences among these sites, keep in mind this quote from the advertising sales director of MTV Europe:

> "An 18-year-old boy in France has more in common with another 18-year-old in Germany than he does with his own parents. We consider them as one nation."

Based on the content and creative strategies of the above Websites, would you say that MTV has expanded this philosophy to include the entire world? Explain your answer. Be sure to discuss the advantages and disadvantages of this approach to youth-oriented advertising.

20-5   ORGANIZING FOR INTERNATIONAL ADVERTISING   (633)

Would you say that the following Website (including its related regional links) reflects a *centralized* or *decentralized* organizational structure? Cite specific examples to support your answer.

Visa   http://www.visa.com

Why do you think Visa chose this organizational strategy for its Website advertising? What are the advantages of this approach? Can you think of any disadvantages?

20-6   GLOBAL PERSPECTIVE: LEVI STRAUSS BEGINS TO THINK GLOBALLY (635)

(*Note to instructors*: We suggest you ask your students to complete Exercise 8-1 before starting this exercise.)

Picking up where Exercise 8-1 left off, let's see how Levi's Website advertising varies depending on which geographical region you live in. First, access the following URL.

Levi.com   http://www.levi.com

As you can see, Levi's gives Web users three regional gateways to choose from — Europe, North America, and Canada. While these three sites share a common design and a significant amount of marketing content, there *is* variation among them. Explore each of these regional sites thoroughly and answer the following questions.

What are the primary differences among these three regional Websites? How do you account for these differences? Conversely, why do you think Levi's made these sites so consistent in form and content?

Assuming that Levi's plans to use Website advertising to reach the Asian market, would you expect it to follow the same Website advertising formula? Aside from obvious language differences, why might Levi's need to take a different approach with respect to its Asian target audience?

20-7   SALES PROMOTION IN INTERNATIONAL MARKETING   (645-8)

To see some real-world examples of sales promotions in international marketing, let's go back to the Yahoo! Website we've visited so many times before.

Yahoo!   http://www.yahoo.com

From the Yahoo! main page, follow the More Yahoos link and scroll down to reveal the World Yahoos list. As you can see, Yahoo! has tailored its service to focus on many geographical regions outside of North America. Of these seven sites (perhaps more by the time you read this), three are English language-based: Yahoo! in Asia, Yahoo! Australia & NZ, and Yahoo! UK & Ireland.

Take a few moments to do some recreational exploring on these three sites. As you peruse each one, pay attention to the advertising banners that appear. Select one banner on each site that reflects a sales promotion conducted by a U.S.-based company.

Identify and describe the promotions you selected. Is each promotion exclusive to a particular geographical area or international in scope?

How might regional differences in economic development, market maturity, consumer perceptions, trade structure, and regulatory environment dictate the international flexibility of these sales promotions?

Considering everything you've learned in this chapter, how do you explain the variation in creative and promotional strategy among the following Mitsubishi Motors Websites? Cite specific examples to support your analysis.

Mitsubishi Motors Australia	http://www.claus-winzer.com/mmal
Mitsubishi Motors Japan	http://www.mitsubishi-motors.co.jp
(Corporate Headquarters)	
Mitsubishi Motors UK	http://www.mitsubishi-cars.co.uk
Mitsubishi Motors USA	http://www.mitsucars.com

Chapter 21: REGULATION OF ADVERTISING AND PROMOTION

21-1 LIQUOR ADVERTISING ON TV: WHAT'S YOUR OPINION? (653)

As you read in the chapter-opening vignette, the Distilled Spirits Council of the United States (DISCUS) voted unanimously in 1996 to overturn its self-imposed ban on broadcast advertising for liquor products. The DISCUS Website highlights the background issues and arguments that led to this historic decision:

DISCUS   http://www.discus.health.org

Familiarize yourself with the DISCUS position on this controversial issue by following the Beverage Alcohol Issues link. Next, prepare a written response expressing your own opinion on this matter. Be sure to summarize the major points on both sides of the debate. What is your stand on each point?

Finally, discuss the potential benefits and pitfalls of the following scenarios: 1) continued industry self-regulation by DISCUS; 2) complete deregulation; and 3) regulation by U.S. government organizations only (i.e., the Federal Trade Commission and/or the Bureau of Alcohol, Tobacco and Firearms).

21-2   SELF REGULATION BY BUSINESSES (657-9)

The **Council of Better Business Bureaus** maintains a truly outstanding Website, much of which is devoted to advertising self-regulation by businesses. We suggest you bookmark the following URL for future reference.

Council of Better Business Bureaus   http://www.bbb.org

Once you've arrived at this site's main page, click on the <u>Advertising Review Programs</u> link. This will give you access to a wealth of information regarding the National Advertising Division, the Children's Advertising Review Unit (CARU), and the **National Advertising Review Board** (NARB). Take a few moments to explore these Web pages.

Once you have a better sense of these resources, click on the <u>NAD Press Releases</u> link. Using as many of these media items as necessary, illustrate the primary advantages of this kind of self-regulation for both advertisers and consumers. How does this type of self-regulation differ from the others discussed in this chapter (see pp. 655-63)? Finally, what are the limitations of voluntary self-regulation by businesses?

21-3   FEDERAL REGULATION OF ADVERTISING: THE FTC (663-76)

Like all major divisions of the U.S. government, the **Federal Trade Commission (FTC)** maintains a public-access informational Website. We suggest you explore this site thoroughly and bookmark the following URL for future reference.

Federal Trade Commission   http://www.ftc.gov

Follow the <u>Consumer Protection</u> link and then click on <u>Advertising Policy Statements and Guidance</u>. Look under the *Dietary Supplement Labels* heading for recent FTC statements on this topic.

Summarize the statement(s) you found. What is the central advertising regulation issue at hand? Based on what you've read, how would you characterize the respective roles of the FTC and the Food and Drug Administration (FDA) with regard to this issue?

Do you think that the regulatory issues surrounding dietary supplement labels reflect the need for federal regulation of advertising, or do you believe that self-regulation would provide adequate consumer protection in this case? Explain your answer.

21-4   DECEPTIVE ADVERTISING (666-7)

Would you say that the following Website advertisement reflects the practice of **puffery**? Use your response to demonstrate your understanding of this term as defined on p. 666.

Prolong   http://www.prolong.com

Describe a hypothetical scenario in which the term **deception** would apply to this product promotion. Again, use your answer to demonstrate your comprehension of the new working definition of this term (see p. 666).

21-5   AFFIRMATIVE DISCLOSURE   (667)

Wal-Mart is one of the largest retail chains in the world, with a reported annual sales income in excess of $100 billion. One of Wal-Mart's longest-running marketing strategies highlighted the fact that all of its products were "Made in the USA." A few years ago, however, a major television newsmagazine exposed this claim as false. Since then, Wal-Mart has adjusted (but by no means abandoned) its emphasis on U.S.-made products. Visit the Website below to find out more about Wal-Mart's new approach.

Wal-Mart   http://www.wal-mart.com

After accessing this site's main page, follow the Corporate Info link and click on Made Right Here. (For more background information, read The Wal-Mart Story.) How would you characterize Wal-Mart's current strategy? In what way does this approach capitalize on the "Made in the USA" image without putting Wal-Mart at risk of making false claims? What are the ethical issues surrounding this tactic?

Finally, how does this case relate to the FTC's **affirmative disclosure** requirement?

21-6   IMC PERSPECTIVE: REGULATION OF TOBACCO ADVERTISING   (675)

R.J. Reynolds (RJR) is one of the largest tobacco companies in the United States. Check out the RJR Website to see what this company is doing to curb teen smoking.

R.J. Reynolds   http://www.greensboro.com/rjrt

Identify and describe RJR's programs aimed at reducing tobacco use among children and teenagers. Given the proposed government restrictions you read about in IMC Perspective 21-3, do you think there are any ulterior motives behind RJR's initiatives? If so, what are they and what are their implications in terms of inhibiting further federal regulation of tobacco advertising? That is, how might these kinds of programs help the tobacco companies reach yet another compromise with the FDA?

Note: For more information on the movement to prevent tobacco advertising aimed at teenagers, check out the National Center for Tobacco-Free Kids Website (http://www.tobaccofreekids.org).

21-7   REGULATION OF CONTESTS AND SWEEPSTAKES   (678-9)

Let's go back to the ContestGuide.com Website you first visited in Exercise 15-8.

ContestGuide.com   http://www.contestguide.com

Choose any three of the contests or sweepstakes featured on this site. Follow the appropriate links to read more about the sales promotions you selected. Identify and describe these promotions.

In each case, has the sponsoring company conformed to the contest and sweepstakes regulations discussed on pp. 678-9? If so, how? If not, what would it need to do in order to comply with these requirements? If any of these regulations are irrelevant, explain why they do not apply in each case.

21-8   REGULATION OF MARKETING ON THE INTERNET   (681)

Just as it has done in the traditional advertising arena, the Council of Better Business Bureaus is leading the way toward responsible self-regulation of Internet advertising. To see this in action, visit BBBOnLine.

BBBOnLine   http://www.bbbonline.org

Summarize the programs and services offered by BBBOnLine. In what way(s) do these initiatives address the proposed restrictions of Internet advertising discussed on p. 681?

Considering all that you have learned in this chapter, are you in favor of continued self-regulation of Website advertising without government involvement, or would you vote to extend the FTC's legal authority to include the Internet? Explain your answer.

Chapter 22: EVALUATING THE SOCIAL, ETHICAL, AND ECONOMIC ASPECTS OF ADVERTISING AND PROMOTION

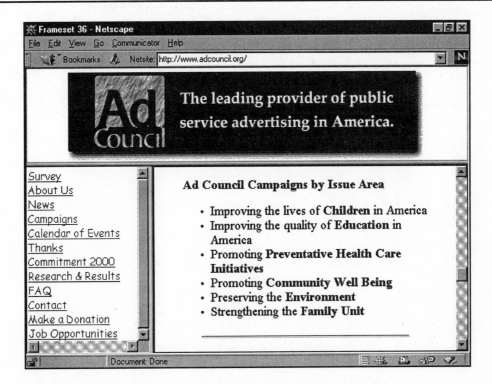

22-1   USING ADVERTISING TO PROMOTE WORTHY CAUSES   (685)

As you read in the chapter-opening vignette, each year the Ad Council creates more than $1 billion of free advertising that promotes worthy causes or addresses critical social problems. To see what the Ad Council has been up to lately, visit its official Website at the following URL.

Ad Council   http://www.adcouncil.org

At the bottom of the main page (in the large frame) you will find a banner promoting one of the Ad Council's current campaigns. Click on this banner and peruse the associated site. What is the central theme of this campaign? How would you describe the appeal and creative strategy used to promote this cause? Do you think this approach is appropriate and effective? Explain your answer.

What are the relative strengths and weaknesses of the Web, television, and print publications as vehicles these kinds of campaigns? Discuss the advantages and disadvantages of each medium.

Finally, think of a worthy cause or social problem that is important to you. Draw up a proposal for an ad campaign to promote change in this area. Be sure to include a memorable campaign slogan.

22-2   ETHICAL PERSPECTIVE: DO BEER COMPANIES TARGET UNDERAGE DRINKERS?   (688)

Consider the following quote from the Beer Institute's advertising and marketing guidelines:

> Beer advertising should not be placed in magazines, newspapers, television programs, or other media where most of the audience is reasonably expected to be below the legal purchase age.

With this idea in mind, explore the following beer advertising Websites:

Budweiser	http://www.budweiser.com
Miller Genuine Draft	http://www.mgdtaproom.com
Molson	http://www.molson.com

In your opinion, do these Websites appeal to people below the legal purchase age for alcoholic beverages? If so, explain why. What are the ethical issues surrounding these kinds of online marketing tactics?

Do you think these sites reflect an irresponsible use of the Internet by the brewing industry? That is, given the fact that a significant percentage of Internet users are children, teens, and college students under the age of 21, do you think these companies should be doing more to protect young people from beer advertising on the Web? Explain your answer.

22-3   ADVERTISING AS OFFENSIVE OR IN BAD TASTE   (690-3)

As you read on p. 690, only in the last few years have traditional media begun accepting ads for condoms, as the AIDS crisis forced them to reconsider their restrictions. But as you'll see, the following Website for Durex, a major condom manufacturer, goes far beyond just promoting safe sex.

Durex   http://www.durex.com

In your opinion, are any elements of this Website offensive or in bad taste? Do you think Durex could ever get away with this kind of marketing strategy on television? Explain your answer.

Up until now, the Web has been an entirely self-regulated communication medium. What do advertisers like Durex stand to lose if proposed government restrictions based on "decency" and "family values" are put in place? What is your personal opinion on this issue? That is, should the Internet continue as a purely self-regulated medium, or should it be subject to the same kinds of federal restrictions as broadcast and print media?

Like its parent cable television network, the Nickelodeon Website features advertising aimed at children.

Nickelodeon   http://www.nick.com

As you explore this site, pay particular attention to the banner ads that appear. What kinds of companies are behind these ads? Is it always apparent from the content of these banners what is actually being sold (or even that they are ads at all)? Explain your answer. How are these interactive ads different from television commercials in terms of their potential effect on children?

Advocates for freedom in advertising might argue that since the Nickelodeon TV network is a pay service and parents must *choose* to have it shown in their homes, parents are also responsible for controlling their children's exposure to the advertising shown on this network. Can you apply this same logic to Nickelodeon's public access Website? Discuss the ethical issues surrounding these youth-oriented marketing strategies.

22-5   ADVERTISING AND STEREOTYPING: TARGETING GAY CONSUMERS   (700)

Planet Out is an online magazine aimed at a gay and lesbian audience. Explore this site thoroughly, paying particular attention to the banner ads that appear.

Planet Out   http://www.planetout.com

Prepare a list of all the advertisers you come across. How many of these products and services seem targeted exclusively at the homosexual population? For those with a more universal appeal, why might these companies have chosen Planet Out as an advertising vehicle? What role did demographic factors *other* than sexual orientation most likely play in this decision?

Do you think any of these advertisements are exploitative? If so, describe them and explain why you think they exploit gays and/or lesbians.

22-6   SOCIAL AND CULTURAL CONSEQUENCES OF ADVERTISING   (694-703)

When you're one of the world's most visible global advertisers, you're bound to run into trouble. Such is the plight of McDonald's, whose public criticism is well documented on the following Website.

McSpotlight   http://www.mcspotlight.org/home.html

Upon accessing this site, follow the <u>Issues</u> link and click on <u>advertising</u>. Summarize the case made against McDonald's advertising practices. Upon which specific social and/or cultural consequences of advertising (see pp. 694-703) are these arguments predicated? What is your personal stand on these issues? Using the McDonald's Website (www.mcdonalds.com) for reference, explain the reasoning behind your response, citing specific examples whenever possible.

Until recently, brewing giants like Anheuser-Busch, Miller, and Molson maintained overwhelming control over the American beer market. In the mid-1980s, however, sales of microbrewed craft beers (also called "boutique" beers) and specialty imports began to surge, causing the large corporate breweries to rethink their marketing strategies. Suddenly, beer drinkers were being drawn in large numbers to new and revived styles that represented a departure in both image and taste from traditional best sellers like Budweiser and Michelob. (For a demonstration of just how big the microbrewing industry has become, do a Yahoo! search using the keywords "brewing company". The results may amaze you.)

To see what one major U.S. brewing company is doing to regain some of its lost market share, check out the Website sponsored by Anheuser-Busch's Specialty Brewing Group.

Anheuser-Busch's Specialty   http://www.hopnotes.com
       Brewing Group

Discuss the implications of this trend (and Anheuser-Busch's reaction) in terms of advertising's economic effects on consumer choice and competition. Does this example reflect the typical competitive scenarios depicted on pp. 704-5? Explain.

Finally, how do the key terms **differentiation**, **barrier to entry**, and **economies of scale** apply in this case?

INDEX OF WEBSITES

The following index contains all of the Websites listed in this exercise book. Corresponding exercise numbers appear in parentheses.

ANTI E-MAIL DIRECT MARKETING GROUPS

CAUCE (14-5).. http://www.cauce.org
spam.abuse.net (14-5) .... http://spam.abuse.net

APPAREL

Benetton (7-7, 12-5).. http://www.benetton.com
Bugle Boy (2-7) .... http://www.bugleboy.com
The Gap (9-8, 13-6, 18-5)... http://www.gap.com
Joe Boxer (8-2) .... http://www.joeboxer.com
Levi Strauss & Co. (16-9)... http://www.levistrauss.com
Levi.com (4-9, 8-1, 20-6)... http://www.levi.com
Tweeds (14-4) .... http://www.tweeds.com

AUTOMAKERS

BMW (8-8)... http://www.bmwusa.com
Chevy Trucks (9-1)... http://www.chevrolet.com/truck/index.htm
General Motors (3-4) .... http://www.gm.com
Infiniti Motors (7-4)... http://www.infinitimotors.com
Mitsubishi Motors Australia (20-8) .... http://www.claus-winzer.com/mmal
Mitsubishi Motors Japan (20-8).................................. http://www.mitsubishi-motors.co.jp
Mitsubishi Motors UK (20-8) .... http://www.mitsubishi-cars.co.uk
Mitsubishi Motors USA (20-8) .... http://www.mitsucars.com
Nissan Global CyberCruise (1-2)................................. http://www.nissan.co.jp
Nissan USA (1-2).. http://www.nissan-usa.com
Saturn (4-1)... http://www.saturn.com
Volkswagen (9-6).. http://www.vw.com

AUTOMOBILE DEALERS

Sayville Ford (1-6)... http://www.fordgiant.com

AUTOMOTIVE PRODUCTS

Prolong (21-4).. http://www.prolong.com
Quaker State (7-3, 15-7) .... http://www.quakerstate.com

BEAUTY, HEALTH, & PERSONAL HYGIENE

Avon (17-7).. http://www.avon.com
The Body Shop (16-5) .... http://www.the-body-shop.com
Durex (22-3) .... http://www.durex.com
Ginsana (9-6) .... http://www.ginsana.com
Just For Men (2-5) .... http://www.justformen.com
LifeStyles (5-8) .... http://www.lifestyles.com
Nicorette (9-2).. http://www.nicorette.com
Oral-B (2-5) .... http://www.oralb.com
OraSure (4-3) .... http://www.orasure.com
Procter & Gamble (15-1) .... http://www.pg.com
Urban Decay (2-5) .... http://www.urbandecay.com

BEVERAGES

Absolut Vodka (8-5)..http://www.absolutvodka.com
Anheuser-Busch's Specialty Brewing
   Group (22-7)..http://www.hopnotes.com
Budweiser (22-2)..http://www.budweiser.com
Coca-Cola Co. (2-2) ....http://www.cocacola.com
"got milk?" (1-5, 8-7)..http://www.got-milk.com
Jolt Cola (Wet Planet Beverages) (8-4) ....http://www.joltcola.com
Krank$_2$0 (6-9)..http://www.rocketcola.com
"Milk, Where's Your Mustache?" (1-5, 6-6).........http://www.whymilk.com
Miller Genuine Draft (22-2) ....http://www.mgdtaproom.com
Molson (22-2)..http://www.molson.com
Pepsi World (2-2, 18-5).......................................http://www.pepsi.com

BRANDS

Fortune Brands (2-9) ....http://www.fortunebrands.com

BROADCAST TELEVISION — NETWORKS

ABC (11-6)...http://www.abc.com
CBS (11-6)..http://www.cbs.com
FOX (3-3, 11-6)...http://www.foxworld.com
NBC (11-6)...http://www.nbc.com

BROADCAST TELEVISION — PROGRAMS

ABC News (11-5)..http://www.abcnews.com
General Hospital (11-3).......................................http://www.port-charles.com/gh
Goosebumps (11-3) ....http://www.foxkids.com/goose.htm
Monday Night Football (11-3) ....http://www.abcmnf.com
Today (11-3, 16-1) ....http://www.msnbc.com/news/TODAY_front.asp

CABLE TELEVISION NETWORKS

BET Networks (2-5)..http://www.betnetworks.com
Channel One (13-10)..http://channelone.com
CNN Interactive (4-5)...http://www.cnn.com
CNN/SI (10-7, 11-1)..http://www.cnnsi.com
Discovery Channel (1-3) ....http://www.discovery.com
ESPN SportsZone (10-7, 11-1).............................http://ESPN.SportsZone.com
The Food Network 11-6).......................................http://www.foodtv.com
Lifetime (11-6) ....http://www.lifetimetv.com
MTV Asia (20-4)...http://www.mtvasia.com
MTV Australia (20-4)..http://www.village.com.au/mtv
MTV Europe (20-4)...http://www.mtveurope.com
MTV Online (USA) (20-4)....................................http://www.mtv.com
Nickelodeon (22-4)..http://www.nick.com
The Travel Channel (11-6) ....http://www.travelchannel.com
Univision (11-6) ....http://www.univision.net

COMPUTER HARDWARE

Apple Computer (9-9, 13-2, 16-4) .... http://www.apple.com
Dell Computer (5-4, 16-7, 17-2) .... http://www.dell.com
Digital Computer (4-8) .... http://www.digital.com
Hewlett-Packard (19-2)... http://www.hp.com
IBM: e-business (19-8) .... http://www.ibm.com/e-business
Micron Electronics (14-10)... http://www.micronpc.com

COMPUTER SOFTWARE & COMPONENTS

Intel (19-3) .... http://www.intel.com
Intel Info for the Channel (15-10)...................................... http://channel.intel.com
Interactive Intelligence (1-6).. http://www.inter-intelli.com
Lotus Development Corp. (14-3, 19-5)................................ http://www.lotus.com
Microsoft (7-6)... http://www.microsoft.com
Netscape (7-6) .... http://www.netscape.com

CONTESTS & SWEEPSTAKES

ContestGuide.com (15-8, 21-7) .... http://www.contestguide.com

COUPONS

America's Coupons (15-6)... http://www.americascoupons.com
Club Coupons (15-6).. http://www.clubcoupons.com
Quick Coupons (15-6).. http://www.qponz.com
Super Saver Grocery Coupons (15-6)................................. http://www.supersaver-coupons.com

CRUISE LINES

Carnival Cruise Lines (9-4)... http://www.carnival.com
Celebrity Cruises (9-4)... http://www.celebrity-cruises.com
Cunard Line (9-4) .... http://www.cunardline.com
Holland America Line (9-4)... http://www.hollandamerica.com
Norwegian Cruise Line (9-4) .... http://www.ncl.com

DIGITAL BROADCAST SATELLITE (DBS)

DBS DISH: Satellite News & Info (11-7)............................ http://www.dbsdish.com
DIRECTV (6-9) .... http://www.directv.com
DISH Network (2-8) .... http://www.dishtv.com

DIRECT MAIL MARKETING

Excalibur Enterprises (14-4).. http://www.excaliburmail.com

DISCOUNT STORES

Wal-Mart (21-5)... http://www.wal-mart.com

ELECTRONICS & ACCESSORIES

Energizer (2-7) .... http://www.energizer.com
Samsung Electronics America (5-1) .... http://www.sosimple.com
Samsung Electronics Co., Ltd. (5-1) .... http://www.sec.samsung.co.kr

EMPLOYMENT

CareerPath.com (4-4) .... http://www.careerpath.com

ENVIRONMENTAL CONSERVATION

Environmental Defense Fund (16-8) .... http://www.edf.org
Greenpeace (16-8) .... http://www.greenpeace.org
Natural Resources Defense Council (16-8) .... http://www.nrdc.org
Sierra Club (16-8) .... http://www.sierraclub.org

FINANCIAL & CREDIT SERVICES

American Express (6-3) .... http://www.americanexpress.com
Discover Card (6-5) .... http://www.discovercard.com
MasterCard (9-5) .... http://www.mastercard.com
Sallie Mae (5-4) .... http://www.salliemae.com
Visa (20-5) .... http://www.visa.com

FIREARMS

Ithaca Gun (4-3) .... http://www.ithacagun.com

FIRE PROTECTION

Kidde Fire Protection (9-2) .... http://www.kidde.com

FOOD INDUSTRY ORGANIZATIONS

California Fresh Tomatoes (1-6) .... http://www.tomato.org
DISCUS (21-1) .... http://www.discus.health.org

FOOD MANUFACTURERS

ABC Girl Scout Cookie Bakers (17-5) .... http://www.girlscoutcookiesabc.com
Archer Daniels Midland Co. (16-10) .... http://www.admworld.com
Ben & Jerry's (16-3) .... http://www.benjerry.com
Butterball (10-6) .... http://www.butterball.com
Chef Boyardee (2-8) .... http://www.chefboy.com
General Mills (3-2, 7-1) .... http://www.generalmills.com
General Mills: You Rule School (7-1) .... http://www.youruleschool.com
Gorton's (4-7) .... http://www.gortons.com
Jelly Belly (3-2) .... http://www.jellybelly.com
Kellogg's (2-3, 7-1) .... http://www.kelloggs.com
Kellogg's Corn Pops (17-3) .... http://www.cornpops.com

Kraft Foods (7-1) .... http://www.kraftfoods.com
Nabisco (1-6) .... http://www.nabisco.com
Newman's Own (5-8, 6-2) .... http://www.newmansown.com
Oscar Mayer (13-4) .... http://www.oscar-mayer.com
Post Cereal (7-1) http://www.post100.com
Quaker Oatmeal Cereals Homepage (14-7) .... http://www.quakeroatmeal.com
Quaker Oats Company Homepage (14-7) .... http://www.quakeroats.com
Ragu Foods (1-3) .... http://www.ragu.com
Smuckers (4-8) .... http://www.smucker.com

FOOTWEAR

Adidas (20-2) .... http://www.adidas.com
Airwalk (1-1) .... http://www.airwalk.com
Fila (6-1) .... http://www.fila.com
Hush Puppies (7-8) .... http://netpad.com/hushpuppies
Mizuno (20-2) .... http://www.mizunousa.com
Nike (6-7, 8-8, 20-2) .... http://www.nike.com
Reebok (1-1) .... http://www.reebok.com

HOME & GARDEN

Aristokraft (5-8) .... http://www.aristokraft.com
Burpee (4-8) .... http://garden.burpee.com
Dirt Devil (7-2) .... http://www.dirtdevil.com
The Gutter Man, Inc. (17-4) .... http://www.gutterman.com
Micro-flo Industries (2-7) .... http://www.micro-flo.com
Orkin (4-2) .... http://www.orkin.com
RotoRooter (9-6) .... http://www.rotorooter.com
Safe-T-Proof (2-5) .... http://www.safe-t-proof.com
Tupperware (17-6) .... http://www.tupperware.com

HOTELS & RESORTS

Helmsley Hotels (6-4) .... http://www.helmsleyhotels.com
Holiday Inn Hotels (2-3) .... http://www.holiday-inn.com
Trump Hotels & Casino Resorts (18-2) .... http://www.trump.com

INDUSTRIAL SUPPLIES & SERVICES

General Electric (19-1) .... http://www.ge.com
The Steel Alliance (4-7) .... http://www.thenewsteel.com
Union Carbide (1-9) .... http://www.unioncarbide.com
Vulcan Industries (17-3) .... http://www.vulcanindustries.com

INFOMERCIALS

tvshopping.com (14-4) .... http://www.tvshopping.com

IN-STORE MEDIA

ActMedia (13-5) .... http://www.actmedia.com

INSURANCE

Allstate Insurance (8-8) ....http://www.allstate.com
Insurance Shopping Network (14-4) http://www.800insureme.com
State Farm Insurance (8-8) http://www1.statefarm.com

INTERNET TV

Enhanced TV (10-1)...http://nc.oracle.com/html/home/index.htm
PC-TV (10-1)..http://www.pctv.com
WebTV (10-1) ....http://www.webtv.com

MAGAZINES — ONLINE (WEBZINES)

Martha Stewart Living (10-8)..http://www.marthastewart.com
PC World's Marketing Site (12-7) ....http://marketing.pcworld.com
PlanetOut (22-5) ....http://www.planetout.com
t@p online network (2-1) ....http://www.taponline.com
UnfURLed (1-10) ....http://www.unfurled.com
Windows95.com (10-10)..http://www.windows95.com

MAGAZINES — PRINT

The Atlantic Monthly (12-5) ....http://www.theatlantic.com
Buzz Magazine (12-2)...http://www.buzzmag.com
Car and Driver (10-8) ....http://www.caranddriver.com
ELLE (12-4)..http://www.ellemag.com
Fathering Magazine (10-8) ....http://www.fathermag.com
Mother Jones (10-8) ....http://www.mojones.com
Nature (12-2)..http://www.nature.com
New York Magazine (12-2)..http://www.newyorkmag.com
Saturday Evening Post (12-4) ....http://www.satevepost.org
Time Magazine (12-3) ....http://www.time.com
Windows Magazine (7-5)...http://www.winmag.com

MEDIA RESEARCH & RATINGS

Graphics, Visualization, & Usability Ctr. (10-3)..................http://www.cc.gatech.edu/gvu
Mediamark Research, Inc. (10-4)...http://www.mediamark.com
Nielsen Media Research (10-3) ....http://www.nielsenmedia.com
Statistical Research, Inc. (11-8)...http://www.sriresearch.com
UltimateTV: Nielsen Ratings (11-8).....................................http://www.ultimatetv.com/news/nielsen

MEDICINE & HEALTH CARE

Advanstar Healthcare Publishing (1-6) ....http://www.modernmedicine.com
Kaiser Permanente (16-2)...http://www.kaiperm.org

MUSIC RETAILERS

CD Universe (14-6) ....http://www.cduniverse.com

NEWSPAPERS

Boston Globe (15-2).. http://www.boston.com/globe
Detroit Free Press (12-8).. http://www.freep.com
National Enquirer (16-2).. http://www.nationalenquirer.com
New York Times (12-9) .... http://www.nytimes.com
San Jose Mercury News (12-8) .... http://www.sjmercury.com
South Florida Sun-Sentinel (12-8).. http://www.sunsentinel.com
Wall Street Journal: Ad Sales (12-10) .... http://adsales.wsj.com
Washington Post (12-8) .... http://www.washingtonpost.com

NOT-FOR-PROFIT ORGANIZATIONS

American Lung Association (6-9).. http://www.lungusa.org
Democratic National Committee (6-8).. http://www.democrats.org
Girl Scouts of the USA (17-5) .... http://www.gsusa.org
MADD (7-2) .... http://www.madd.org
Make-A-Wish Foundation (9-2) .... http://www.wish.org
National Center for Tobacco-Free Kids (21-6).. http://www.tobaccofreekids.org
United Way (16-2) .... http://www.unitedway.org

OFFICE SUPPLIES

Staples (15-3).. http://www.staples.com

ONLINE SERVICES

America Online (12-1).. http://www.aol.com
CompuServe (12-1).. http://world.compuserve.com
Prodigy (12-1).. http://www.prodigy.com

ONLINE SHOPPING MALLS

Cybershop (14-1).. http://209.67.3.40/store/store.hmx
iMALL (14-1).. http://www.imall.com
The Internet Mall (14-1) .... http://www.internetmall.com

PACKAGING

STORA Paperboard (1-6) .... http://www.stora-paperboard.com
Ziploc (2-8).. http://www.ziploc.com

PET PRODUCTS

Iams (4-2).. http://www.iams.com
Milk-Bone (9-2).. http://www.milkbone.com

PHOTOCOPYING & DIGITAL IMAGING

Canon (20-3).. http://www.canon.com
Xerox (19-7) .... http://www.xerox.com

PHOTOGRAPHY

Kodak Picture Network (4-7) .... http://www.kodakpicturenetwork.com

PRESCRIPTION DRUGS

Allegra (14-10) .... http://www.ahhh-allegra.com
Claritin (10-6) .... http://www.allergy-relief.com
INFeD (17-3) .... http://www.infed.com

PRESS RELEASE SERVICES

PR Newswire (16-6) .... http://www.prnewswire.com
Yahoo!: PR Newswire (1-7) .... http://biz.yahoo.com/prnews

PROMOTIONAL PRODUCTS MARKETING

PPA's Promotion Clinic (13-7) .... http://www.promotion-clinic.ppa.org

PUBLISHERS & AUTHORS

Dr. Seuss (9-6) .... http://www.randomhouse.com/seussville
Hallmark (5-8, 8-8) .... http://www.hallmark.com

RADIO

Radio Advertising Bureau (11-9, 11-10) .... http://www.rab.com

RESTAURANTS

Burger King (8-3) .... http://www.burgerking.com
Kentucky Fried Chicken (8-9) .... http://www.kentuckyfriedchicken.com
McDonald's (4-10, 8-9, 10-9) .... http://www.mcdonalds.com
McSpotlight (22-6) .... http://www.mcspotlight.org/home.html
Subway (8-9) .... http://www.subway.com
Taco Bell (8-9) .... http://www.tacobell.com
Wendy's (5-2) .... http://www.wendys.com

SHIPPING & MAILING SERVICES

Airborne Express (17-3) .... http://www.airborne-express.com
Paul Arpin Van Lines (2-8) .... http://www.paularpin.com

SPORTS — PROFESSIONAL ORGANIZATIONS

Ladies Professional Golf Association (15-9) .... http://www.lpga.com
NASCAR (18-1) .... http://www.nascar.com
Women's NBA (16-2) .... http://www.wnba.com

SPORTS – TEAMS & ATHLETES

Grant Hill (6-1) .... http://www.granthill.com
New York Yankees (1-3) .... http://www.yankees.com

TAX SERVICES

Secure Tax (10-6) .... http://www.securetax.com

TELECOMMUNICATIONS

Cellular One (2-5) .... http://www.cellularone.com
MCI (8-10, 11-4, 19-6) .... http://www.mci.com
Sprint (6-3) .... http://www.sprint.com/index.html

TOBACCO COMPANIES

R.J. Reynolds (21-6) .... http://www.greensboro.com/rjrt

TOURIST ATTRACTIONS

Graceland (4-3) .... http://www.elvis-presley.com
Rock & Roll Hall of Fame (10-2) .... http://www.rockhall.com
San Diego Zoo (1-9, 7-9) .... http://www.sandiegozoo.org

TRAVEL SERVICES

Accessibility Travel (2-5) .... http://www.disabled-travel.com

U.S. ARMED FORCES RECRUITING

U.S. Air Force (9-3) .... http://www.airforce.com
U.S. Army (1-9, 9-3) .... http://www.goarmy.com
U.S. Navy (7-2, 9-3) .... http://www.navy.com

U.S. GOVERNMENT AGENCIES

Federal Trade Commission (21-3) .... http://www.ftc.gov

VIDEO GAMES

LucasArts (15-5) .... http://www.lucasarts.com
Mindscape Games: Creatures (4-2) .... http://creatures.mindscape.com

WATCHES

Omega (2-4) .... http://www.omega.ch
Swatch (2-4) .... http://www.swatch.com
Timex (2-4, 8-8) .... http://www.timex.com
Vision Watch (2-4) .... http://www.visionwatch.com

WEIGHT LOSS

Jenny Craig (1-9) .... http://www.jennycraig.com

WORLD WIDE WEB SEARCH ENGINES

Alta Vista..http://www.altavista.digital.com
BizWeb ....http://www.bizweb.com
Excite! ....http://www.excite.com
Infoseek ....http://www.infoseek.com
Lycos ....http://www.lycos.com
Magellan ....http://www.mckinley.com
Open Text Index ....http://index.opentext.net
WebCrawler..http://www.webcrawler.com
Yahoo! ....http://www.yahoo.com

YELLOW PAGES

BigYellow (13-8)..http://www1.bigyellow.com